TEENAGE WO...
All-in-One Dia...
and Su...

ROS ASQUITH

<u>**N.B.**</u> This book is MAGIC!

Open it at random.

Select a word within 10 lines from the top, and within the first 10 words of the line. MAKE A NOTE OF IT. Then: double the number of the page, multiply the result by 5, add 30, add the number of the line you selected, add 5, multiply by 10, add the number of the word in the line, take away 350, and the remainder will give you the page number, line and word in order!

PICCADILLY PRESS · LONDON

TO ALL TEENAGE WORRIERS

Phototypeset and designed by Finn Lewis
Printed and bound in India by Thomson Press
for the publishers, Piccadilly Press Ltd.,
5 Castle Road, London NW1 8PR

A catalogue record for this book is available
from the British Library.

ISBN: 1 85340 365 2

Ros Asquith lives in North London. Her cartoon strip, *Doris*,
appears weekly in the *Guardian* and she draws regularly for *She*.
Piccadilly Press published her best-seller, *I Was A Teenager Worrier*.
Also by Ros Asquith: *Baby!* (Optima), *Green!* (Pandora), *Babies!*
and *Toddler!* (Fontana).

Reprinted 1993
This edition, 1995

This is a book for doodling on. Here is my ickle brother's portrait of me

This book belongs to

Name...

Address..

....

NHS No...

Age..

Sex..

OK clever clogs, this means 'gender'
so don't put 'yes please' or 'as
often as poss' Etck. Etck.
Add School and other V. Boring
details. Etck.

1

Sluggs Comprehensive,
Rancid Rd,
London,
England,
Teeny Britain,
Europe (pull the other one),
The World,
The Solar System,
The Galaxy,
The Universe,
The Cosmos,
Infinity.

← Ye school spider

Still the 20th Century

Dear Fiends (sorry there should be an r in there),
Are you still Worried? I am, and if I don't Worry for a few seconds, I Worry that I'm getting Alzheimer's disease and have lost Grip on Reality. Sometimes I console myself by thinking about all those people who don't look as if they Worry and nothing awful happens to them, does it? Then I think, they DO Worry, it's just that their faces know how to enjoy themselves without them. Although Worry started at the Dawn of Time, Anxiety is a V 20th Century phenomenon. It is worse than Worry and makes you V Anxious thinking about it.

When I was little (before I got legs like a giraffe's and a neck like the Post Office Tower, boo hoo, yearn for Lost Yoof, Golden Age, Garden of Eden, Innocent Pleasures, Etck Etck) I always wanted a Key-To-The-Universe Walkman that would whisper the Secrets of Everything In The World, ie how to make tons of dosh or what the teachers had been doing with their partners that night (though I could usually guess the latter with a swift glance at their depressed expressions, ie not much). Also to write my V dark secrets, hopes, fears, Emergency Doctor's phone no in case I cut my knee Etck. But now I am Grown Old and have put away Childish Things (except my teddy, bunny

3

rabbit slippers, pony books, jigsaws, farting cushion, plastic spiders Etck) I find I still pine for such a volume. If I ever find it - and since my only chance of a job will be pyramid selling of CD Rom Encyclopaedias, anything is possible - I will let you know.

Meanwhile, since existence on planet Earth continues to be a Writhing mass of Worries - and since I now have to spend at least an hour every week doing schoolwork in between examining my spots, measuring my hooter Etck and therefore do not have time to write the blockbuster I had intended - here is a V Quickly cobbled together (I mean, V Painstakingly researched) little gift book for you to doodle on, make paper aeroplanes out of, send undying messages of Lurve to Evil Sex Machines from Hell Who Don't Care on Etck Etck.

↑
Ye
School
Spider's
FRIEND

As you will see, I have left lots of blank space for you to write on because this is the cheapest (I mean most sensible) way to do a diary. It's a V Clever diary because you can start it whenever you buy the book, like in October or May instead of on Jan 1st. If you start a diary on Jan 1st it's no good because you have always stopped writing in it by Jan 15th and then you spend the rest of the year harbouring a nagging sense of failure and deciding your next Year's Resolution will be to keep up your diary, instead of useful things like Saving the Planet or researching Zit Cures Etck for the Teenage Think Tank.

I would like to take this opportunity (as I will doubtless remark when modestly accepting the Noble Prize for Lichrechure) to thank my V Good new Frend RUTH WILLIAMS (she is V.Modest, so I won't mention the name RUTH WILLIAMS again, except to say that RUTH WILLIAMS has V kindly found out lots of V useful addresses of people to write to and organisations to join,

4

lobby Etck. if you are worried about WAR, SEX, HEALTH, DISEASE, ILLNESS, THE COMMON COLD (sorry, I'm writing this in the Hay Fever season, so I got a bit carried away there), the ENVIRONMENT, SEX, (did I mention that already? - I'm going to be a Nun anyway so it doesn't worry me), HOW TO GET A JOB (aaaaaaaaarg) or where you can learn SPORTS (campaign for Girls Football so the next generation will not suffer as I have done, fume fume), CRAFTS (I wouldn't show Daniel my etchings anyway, not even for a weekend in Paris above a Pain au Fudge shop). A V Big thank you to RUTH WILLIAMS and anybody who has not clocked her name definitely has Alzheimer's.

So, dear reader(s) - I put in the plural, modestly, in case my Mother and my big brother both buy this book - don't blame me, blame RUTH WILLIAMS if she has left out your V Favourite activity. Tragically, as far as I know, there is still no 'Nosepickers Anonymous', nor, shockingly, any Support Groups for Toenail Collectors, Fudge Fanatics, Teen Worriers who were born on Dec 25 and who therefore have less Birthday presents than their siblings, or The Children of Parents who are Trying to Kick the Nicotine Chewing Gum Habit (my adored father's intricate sculptures in this stuff stick to everything you own. He says it is better than smoking but I am beginning to wonder). There is still no address either for CHAP (The Campaign for Hairy Armpits) or the TTT (Teenage Think Tank), so pleeeese write to your MP or the PM (see address section) demanding a TEENAGE THINK TANK now, so that our once Great nation can benefit from all our V brill ideaz and so that we can all get jobs, dosh, houses Etck. (Not me, I will live in a cave tending wounded creatures, as long as they do not include my friend Aggy or my Dad, and meditating on the Eternal Verities.)

↑
Ye
School
Spider's
Friend's
Friend

TEENAGE WORRIER'S FRIEND

I have also put in LETTY CHUBB'S Monthly Guide and a few ideaz, puzzles, jokes Etck to cheer you up between Worries. How hard is the life of the 20th Century Teenager! (Although of course we are vv privileged and don't know how lucky we are Etck Etck guilt lash).

Whoops, here comes Miss Farthing (the one who hates it if we drop our aitches, specially when writing her name) and I am supposed to be writing an essay on Crop Rotation (one printer's error and the whole picture changes, though it might be a very good thing for the crops). Perhaps we need a section on Vowel Movements.

Letty Chubb

Scarlett Jane Chubb

Ye School Spider's Friend's Friend's Friend

PS I am still VVV worried about my Nose, my eyebrows (I think they are starting to meet in the middle), my name, Granny Chubb (I caught her eating cat food again last week because it's cheaper), my Father (who is up to two packs of Nicotine gum a day), my ickle brother Benjy (who is V scared of the Teddy Bear pattern on his curtains), the fact that I still need to use a magnifying glass when looking at my bra zone, my frendz Hazel and Aggy and - Daniel - but that's another story. It is only Rover who keeps me sane.

Rover - my Sanity Module

LIST YOUR WORST FEARS AND WORRIES HERE

Worst worries   Argghh!

Biggest fears   Wooooooo!

Best Frendz

People I LURVE

INACTIVITY SECTION

Draw your family (Ho ho don't let them see Etck)

Draw your pets

I have drawn my
cat Rover to cheer
you up if you
don't have a
pet.

QUIZ *Are you a teenage worrier?*

Answer the following questions by ticking the appropriate box.

VVV Worried
VV Worried
V Worried
Worried
Not Worried
HAPPY about

Worry worry worry

1. Your Health?
2. Your Family's Health?
3. Your looks?
4. Your family's looks?
5. The environment?
6. Poverty?
7. World Peace?
8. Schoolwork?
9. Bullying?
10. Exams?
11. Your Bra or Willy size?
12. Food?
13. The number thirteen?
14. Money?
15. What kind of job you'll get?
16. Sex?
17. Friends?
18. The End of the World?
19. The End of Your Nose?
20. Dandruff?
21. Spots?
22. The weather?
23. Your Personality?
24. Your Pet's Personality?

Answers on page 12

10

INACTIVITY SECTION

	V V V Worried	V V Worried	V Worried	Worried	Not Worried	HAPPY about
1	☐	☐	☐	☐	☐	☐
2	☐	☐	☐	☐	☐	☐
3	☐	☐	☐	☐	☐	☐
4	☐	☐	☐	☐	☐	☐
5	☐	☐	☐	☐	☐	☐
6	☐	☐	☐	☐	☐	☐
7	☐	☐	☐	☐	☐	☐
8	☐	☐	☐	☐	☐	☐
9	☐	☐	☐	☐	☐	☐
10	☐	☐	☐	☐	☐	☐
11	☐	☐	☐	☐	☐	☐
12	☐	☐	☐	☐	☐	☐
13	☐	☐	☐	☐	☐	☐
14	☐	☐	☐	☐	☐	☐
15	☐	☐	☐	☐	☐	☐
16	☐	☐	☐	☐	☐	☐
17	☐	☐	☐	☐	☐	☐
18	☐	☐	☐	☐	☐	☐
19	☐	☐	☐	☐	☐	☐
20	☐	☐	☐	☐	☐	☐
21	☐	☐	☐	☐	☐	☐
22	☐	☐	☐	☐	☐	☐
23	☐	☐	☐	☐	☐	☐
24	☐	☐	☐	☐	☐	☐

ANSWERS TO TEENAGE WORRIER QUIZ

Score 10 for *VVV Worried*, 8 for *VV Worried*,
6 for *V Worried*, 4 for *Worried*, 2 for *Not Worried*
and 0 for *HAPPY about*.

235-240. *You are Right to be Worried. See your Doctor.
NB: If you scored 10 on question 22, see an analyst. Also
see an analyst if you scored 10 on question 24 (unless you
own a rotweiller).*

194-234. *My score, actually. You are a Teenage Worrier. It's
hard, but always remember, when one door closes, another
door closes.*

144-193. *I am V worried that I didn't get this score or lower,
because you are still a Teenage Worrier, so what does that
make me? However, you are on the road to sanity. Try to
relax and get out of yourself occasionally, by taking a nap,
or Time Travelling.*

96-143. *Yes, you are a Teenage Worrier, but you are able to
preserve a perspective on Life's Roller Coaster. Its ups and
downs will carry you - um - Up and Down but you will be
able to see the funny side in between leaning over the brown
paper bag.*

44-95. *I hate to say this, because you may think you are a
Worrier. But by the Letty Chubb Astronome of Teenage
Worry, you are not. Congratulations. Go into the
Government, where nobody worries about anything. Yeeech.*

0-43. *Liar. Or, as the MP who was accused of calling
another MP a liar once said in Parliament, 'I called the
Honourable gentleman a liar it is true and I am sorry for
it. The Honourable gentleman may put in the
punctuation.'*

JOIN THE DOTS

Is fig 1 (a) A banana and two apples? (b) A Big willy?
(c) An abstract doodle

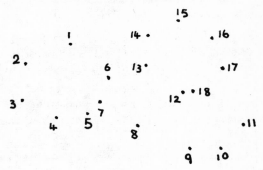

Is fig 2 (a) A nice peach? (b) A Big bottom?
(c) An abstract doodle?

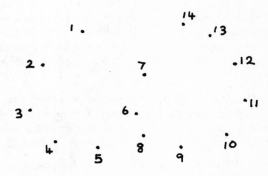

What do you think it is?
Answers on p. 20

13

TEEN WORRIER'S ROOM

*Here is a teenage worrier's bedroom before and after
tidying up. Can you spot 10 differences?
And can you spot which is the BEFORE
and which is the AFTER picture?*

Answers on page 20....

CIRCLE YOUR DREAM LURVE
(and who you would like to look like)

If you circled A or F you are VV predictable and should retire to consider the Mysteries of the Soul, the Importance of the Intellect, Personality, Deeper Values Etck Etck.

CIRCLE THE PERSON MOST LIKE YOU

If you circled B can I have your phone number? If you circled G or A, consult a therapist regarding possible low self-esteem.

HERE IS A TYPICAL TEENAGE WORRIER BEFORE AND AFTER DECIDING WHAT TO WEAR TO MEET A DREAM DATE

*Can you pluke (I mean spot) which is the 'BEFORE'
and which is the 'AFTER' picture?
And can you spot Ten differences?*

Answers on page 21...

Answers to JOIN THE DOTS

If you answered (a) you are v. interested in food, (b) you are v. interested in naughty bits, (c) is right. Otherwise my publishers will be sued.

Answers to BEDROOM

The Second picture is the BEFORE picture.

The Ten Differences.

1. She has straightened her poster of BEAN, forgetting that it was covering her last year's poster of HUNK.

2. She has removed six T-shirts from under her bed, to reveal eighteen odd socks.

3. She has attempted to remove the mugs from her bedside table, but has been put off by their green fur jackets, so she has straightened them a little, instead.

4. She has shoved the six T-shirts that were under the bed into the chest of drawers, which now won't close.

5. She has painted a little design on the lampshade, carefully choosing a non-inflammable lightshade proof paint (as she is a worrier) but neglecting the drips.

6. She has re-arranged her shoe sculpture.

7. She has re-arranged her notice board.

8. She has emptied a boxful of letters and photos onto her bed in order to sort through them.

9. She has filled the previously empty waste paper basket with old letters from her ex-Boyfriend who went off into the sunset with the milkman.

10. She has become sentimental over some of the

letters and pinned them in a rather fetching arrangement on her leggings, as a Statement.

Answers to DREAM DATE

The FIRST picture is the BEFORE picture.

The Ten Differences

1. She has changed her new jeans for older, more casual ones.
2. She has combed a few stray hairs over her nose, to look carefree.
3. She has foolishly placed a plaster over her biggest spot, unwittingly drawing attention to it.
4. She is slouching, as her date is four inches shorter than she is.
5. She has added a badge, to show she is committed to Animal Rights, as her date is Vegetarian, and, she hopes, an Animal...
6. She has removed her platform shoes, for the same reason as 4. above.
7. She has tried to pluck her eyebrows, resulting in multiple contusions.
8. She has washed her hair, forgetting, as she always does, that this renders it attractive only to those contemplating washing up after cooking omelettes and seeking a suitable tool.
9. She has taken her copy of Smirk Magazine out of her shoulder bag and replaced it with a copy of 'War and Peace', which is much heavier, to convince her date that she is an Intellectual.
10. Her mascara has run a mite (or amok), as she has been crying about her hair.

SUN SIGNS

Er, serious astrologers, (if that's not a contradiction in terms) look at loads of other things, like RISING signs Etck and whether yr MOON was in URANUS (ho ho)

Astrology began in Mesopotania many thousands of years ago, so if Granny Chubb, who always says that Age Breeds Wisdom, is anyone to go by then there might be something in it. I myself am extremely sceptical, though I must admit I do turn to the horoscope page in *Smirk* first every week, and prefer to check my horoscope for the day before doing anything really important, like going out of the house, or getting up. But you can do a quick check with L.Chubb's definitive list below, to see how right astrology is for you and you frendz.

	YOU	YOUR FRENDZ
ARIES	Dynamic, headstrong, brave	Impatient, selfish, pushy
TAURUS (Moi!)	Very patient, reliable, sensual, thoughtful, calm	Plodding, stubborn, boring
GEMINI	Versatile, witty, clever	Two-faced, scatty, untidy
CANCER	Sensitive, caring, protective	Moody, cautious, homely
LEO	Enthusiastic, fun-loving, generous	Show off, bossy, proud
VIRGO	Diligent, precise, clever	Fussy, critical, anxious

LIBRA	Perfectionist, calm, charming	Indecisive, flirtatious, discontented
SCORPIO	Analytical, strong-willed, passionate	Jealous, obsessive, (esp with sex!) intense
SAGITTARIUS	Optimistic, honest, opinionated	Restless, tactless, forever bored
CAPRICORN	V. organized, ambitious, reliable	Boring, cautious, hard to relax
AQUARIUS	Independent, determined, inventive	Weird, rebellious, unpredictable
PISCES	Kind, gentle, imaginative	Supersensitive, indecisive, dippy

This goes to prove as far as I am concerned that Horoscopes are in the eye of the beholder Etck. Anyway, apparently astral bodies have moved a few miles since charts were invented, so now Taurus is Gemini ... or is it the other way round? Wish I could twine myself round the astral body of Daniel (sob, grrrrr).

POINT
HORROR
SCOPES

V. Nice Cake →

FOOD, GLORIOUS FOOD

(slurp)

It's a v.v.v. major worry that teenagers with perfect hour-glass figures like Hazel spend their time trying to get rid of their non-existent flabby bits. This is why today's Yoof are plagued by lots of nasty illnesses like anorexia and bulimia. It is also V.V. worrying that magazines such as *Smirk, Tru-Luv* and *Teenybop* are irresponsible enough to encourage them by stuffing their pages full of wafer-thin models and devoting endless column inches to losing weight.

It's also v.v.v. boring for people like moi who eat as much Plumpo as they can and still get mistaken for a bamboo stick (though not for a wafer-thin model alas) and told by all their more generously proportioned frendz to eat more. There aren't any articles on increasing weight are there? V. Unfair. I'm going to campaign to my MP about giving magazine discounts to people for whom half the articles are irrelevant. In the meantime I take it upon myself to redress the balance so for all thin, puny teenage worriers, here is L. Chubb's 10 point guide to being fat:

HOW TO BE FAT

1. Eat 36 Mars Bars, have high fat everything and chips each day.
2. Don't worry about the heart attack you'll probably get from eating the above (if you worry, all the little nervous habits related to it – like biting nails and fidgeting – can burn up zillions of calories).
3. Eat lots of pasta (look at Pavarotti). That's what I thought anyway. I went through a stage of eating pasta,

L. chubb's fave food is FUDGE

pasta, pasta until my brother Ashley said I looked like pasta – a string of spaghetti.

4. Do masses of sport which will help you build up lots of muscles. If you want fat instead of muscles you could then become a couch potato and watch the muscle turn to fat.

5. Wear horizontal stripes, or v. baggy shirts so you can wear a lot of padding underneath. Avoid Lycra.

6. Make sure your family celebrates all the festivals (like Christmas and Thanksgiving and Easter and Passover and Birthdays) where everybody spends their time eating (you'll also get more presents and lots more holidays from school as a bonus).

7. Keep the odd skeleton in the cupboard so you'll look fat in comparison (joke!).

8. Go to a fair or somewhere where they have those distorting mirrors (make sure you look in the right mirror).

9. Resign yourself to the fact that your doctor will tell you there's nothing you can do about it every time you visit the surgery – do the above anyway (and don't worry about the doc threatening to strike you off after the tenth visit in two weeks – see point 2).

10. Er ... can't think of anything else.

N.B. NEVER have salad without a little sprinkle of cream & sugar

But I'm not like those *Smirk* Etck writers and ignore some people completely. This new scientific breakthrough is based on my extensive observational research. I am thinking of selling it to magazines, FATTYWATCHERS etck. for loads of money but you get it for just £3.99 (or whatever the price of this book is). ← v. cheap, please buy 2 copies

L. CHUBB'S THEORY ON HOW TO LOSE WEIGHT

(or wot a waste of time Etck. You cld be reading a NOVEL)

Teenage Worriers who think they're fat are v.v.v. boring and spend their *entire* life thinking about what foods they *can't* eat and how much more yummy these things are than what they *can* eat – rather than contemplating more interesting things like Einstein's Theory of Relativity or why it is that things they *can* eat always seem to make them fart and burp a lot. If you think about Tasting the Forbidden Fruits (except that fruit is about the only thing which isn't forbidden) for long enough, then it's only human to yield to temptation sooner or later. As you're thinking about them *all day and night,* the fact that you only taste them about thirty times a day doesn't seem to be that often. Other people who are not worried about their weight taste these supposedly-fattening things about three times a day. So: if you want to be thin *don't* go on a diet or deny yourself scrumptious food of any kind.

worry worry...

Anyway lots of Teenage Worriers who think they're fat actually have distorted vision so here's a test to see whether you really are fat or whether you need a trip to the optician. If you score 10 out of 10 then you probably are a teeny bit overweight – but always check with your doctor first.

1. You can't fit into a seat at the cinema. *(with one foot)*
2. The scales break when you stand on them.
3. You can see more than ten rolls of flab on your stomach when you sit down.
4. You can't see your toes when you're standing up – even when leaning forward. *← remove shoes first*
5. Your bed keeps on breaking. *← Disregard if reason for collapse is NOOKY (chance wld be a fine thing).*

26

6. You eat more than six square meals a day – and snack in between.

7. You've got more chins than you can count on one hand.

8. You have to pay for excess luggage on the plane when you've only got one small bag.

9. Your lips can't meet the Boy of Your Dreams' when you're standing up.

10. You think that Pavarotti looks thin.

And just to prove, once more, that this book isn't thinist:

HOW TO TELL IF YOU'RE VERY THIN – Look in mirror. If you can't see yourself then use these tips to double check:

1. You intend to join L Chubb's campaign for magazine discounts.

2. You avoid anything which has a "low calorie" or "low fat" label on it.

3. You're always being told you're too thin (which is V.V.V.rude because not many people would go up to someone and tell them they were too fat – but for some reason they feel entitled to insult you if you're the opposite).

4. You find unpadded chairs extremely uncomfortable.

5. You don't know why everybody complains about waif-like models.

6. The pointer doesn't move when you get on the scales.

7. You can see a bulge in your stomach when you've swallowed something.

8. Boyz find you too uncomfortable to hug (sob, sob).

9. You always have to wear a belt or braces to prevent your underwear being exposed.

10. You get out of the bath before letting the water out for fear of being washed down the plug hole.

EAT MORE FUDGE

PSYCHOLOGICAL TEST

This is a test that my friend Hazel tried on me and Aggie the other day. It's v silly, but I need to fill up more pages of this book to make it fatter and so people are more likely to buy it and I get more money (joke). Also see my Alternative Version, later, to prove I don't buy any of this stuff (ahem).

You're supposed to close your eyes and concentrate hard. This is difficult if you're doing this on your own as then you won't be able to read what you should be thinking about. You could get a friend to read it out to you. If you're friendless then you could read through it and try to remember what you're meant to be doing, but then you'd have to have a V.V.V. good memory. Worry, Worry. I don't suppose it would matter too much if you had your eyes open.

Are you sitting comfortably? Then we'll begin. (This is a phrase that my father still uses. It comes from some children's radio programme that he used to listen to when he was Yooful writer – he wasn't a child and hadn't got children, but Writers like my father spend a long time listening to the radio).

INACTIVITY SECTION

1. You go for a walk in the forest. Imagine the kind of forest you're in. Is it light or dark? Is it airy? Are the trees tall or stunted?

stunted trees, dark, damp

2. What is the path like? Is it winding, is it straight? Does it go up and down or is it level? Are there obstacles? Is there a path at all?

winding, level, obstacles (trees fallen)

3. You come across a plastic bucket. What do you do with it?

Walk around it

4. You're walking along and suddenly you come across a bear. How do you react?

scream & run

5. You carry on walking. Then you come to a body of water. Describe the water and what you do when you see it.

brook, dirty leaves in carry on walking alongside

6. A little while later, and you're walking on. There is a wall blocking your way. What do you do?

Change directions

N.B. No pictures on this page so you KNOW it is V. Imp to keep yr MiND crystal clear, uncluttered, E tck.

EXPERT PSYCHOLOGICAL ANALYSIS
(according to Hazel anyway)

1. The forest refers to how you think of life. This means that if it is light and breezy then you think that life is light and breezy, if it is mysterious then you think that life is mysterious. My forest was creepy with owls and bats in it, so I suppose that means that my life is full of creeps and owls and bats. Shucks. Hazel said that when she did it, her forest was a very hot jungle in Africa and that that means her life is hot, as in great. I think it means her life is hot, as in the opposite of cold, which means humid and lethargic too.

2. The path refers to what you make of life. I suppose this means that if it's straight then your life is easy – unless you had a few rocks in the way of the path. I think this is a bit unfair, because obviously if you're in a creepy, dark forest like mine in the first place, then your path will creep round things and be dark, and you come across puddles and slugs and keep losing your way. Still, as Aggie didn't have a path at all and was fighting her way through the nettles, I suppose it could be worse (she said this meant her life was an adventure. I didn't like to disillusion her).

3. The plastic bucket is your friends. Or to be precise, how you treat your friends. If you pick it up and keep it with you for the rest of your walk, then you look after friendships and keep them with you. I picked mine up, and I don't know what I did with it, but 't certainly disappeared from my hand by the end of the walk, so maybe my friendships just evaporate. At least I didn't leave the bucket where it was, or kick it away. But if you

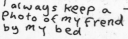

I always keep a photo of my frend by my bed

did, prob just means yr in a Bad Mood. Or wanted a nice galvanised steel bucket. Why not?

4. The bear refers to how you deal with problems. If you run away or climb up a tree immediately then it bodes badly. Naturally, that's what I did.

5. The water refers to your passions. So if your water is a little puddle then bad luck! If your water is a large lake then you obviously have passions, but unless you plunge into it and go for a swim then you're not necessarily very passionate (says Hazel). My water was a raindrop. However, as my Sun sign (Taurus) says I'm very sensual, I'm taking that with a pinch of salt (maybe the salt came from Aggie's ocean – even looking at the sea makes her feel sick! Heh, Heh!). I won't tell you what Hazel's water was (grrr), but she must have been lying.

6. The wall refers to what you think of the after life. If you climbed over the wall, it means you believe in an after life, though I didn't think I did really.

Now read the REALLY <u>REAL</u> Answers and then cheer self up with L Chubb's Alternative Quizzo.

L Chubb's alternative answers:

1. If you think the forest is light and breezy, you're in a meadow. A forest is a place with a lot of *trees* in, dumbo. You know, *shady*. Or maybe you are just v.v. optimistic (unlike moi, sob).

2. V.V. unfair. *All* forests have winding paths unless planted by National Trust, in which case not real forests and not worthy of Teen Worrier's imagination.

3. Plastic bucket? My Frendz?! Much as I wld like them to put same over *head* once in a while, I find this v. insulting.

4. Anyone who does not flee from a bear (especially when armed only with a bucket), needs help fast. What are you expected to do? Invite it to a Teddy Bear's picnic?

5. Non swimmers are at a serious disadvantage here. I *know* vast oceans are supposed to be sexy Etck. But why would I meet them in a forest?

6. I did climb the wall, but it was exactly the same the other side. If this is the after life, you can keep it till, well, After Life.

NB

My favourite people go through v. murky woods through tangled briars kicking any buckets they meet hanging about on the way. They sock the bear (why should you be nice to a problem?), paddle in a puddle and decide it's time to turn back when they see the wall. Then they go home to a nice hot bath, crumpet Etck. Pausing only to muse why psychotherapists devise questionnaires to make the reader v. miserable, inadequate, Etck, Etck.

Here's *my* version

You are in yr room.
1. Is it bright & breezy or fetid with old socks?

2. You go to another room. Is it the bathroom or the kitchen or the living room? (If you're lucky enough to have all these).

3. You go on the stairs. Do they go up? Or down?

4. You see a plastic bucket. What do you do?

5. You see a bear. What is your response?

6. You find some water. Describe it.

7. And now you see a wall. Is there anything you do *now*?

MOMENT OF TRUTH
(part 2 - the real thing)

TEENAGE WORRIER'S FRIEND

Answers:

1. If your room is bright and breezy it means you are a tidy Teenage Worrier. If it is fetid Etck it means you are an UNtidy Teenage Worrier. Both types are fine by moi.

2. If you go to the bathroom you are probably a) Getting ready to go out with Person of Dreams. b) Needing a pee. If you choose kitchen you are hungry. If you choose living room you are in mood for TV.

3. Stairs go up *and* down. Both answers are correct.

4. It depends where the bucket is. If it was under a drip I hope you left it there. Unless the drip was your younger sibling using it as loo.

5. I hope you picked the bear up and put it on your sibling's bed where it belongs. Or your own bed (I have only 16 teddies, but I know some Teen Worriers have hundreds).

6. The water is most likely a drip (see 4 above). Unless imminent danger threatens, leave until suitable adult notices. Otherwise you may have to call plumber instead of involving yourself in useful tasks like picking fluff out of toes Etck. Water could be bath which you forgot you ran and is now stone cold or bott of mineral water as your parent is trying to kick booze and will not stoop to using tap. (All answers are correct).

7. A wall? Why not? You are in a house aren't you?

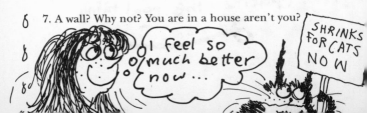

BOYZ QUIZ ← Er 'DATES' QUIZ, really.

I have devised a revealing quiz which will tell you if the BYL (Boy You Like) is also a BLY (Boy who Likes You). This could save you many hours of anguish and trauma. (If you have Urges for Girlz rather than Boyz, like my frend Hazel, then substitute B for G, and he for she and him for her Etck.)

You have gone out for the evening to the cinema:

1. How come you're at the cinema with BYL:
(a) He asked you if you'd like to go (and which film you'd prefer to see)?
(b) He was going with your best friend, but you told him she was ill and he could take you instead?
(c) You didn't actually go with BYL – he happens to be sitting in the next door seat?

2. You have a huge wart on the tip of your nose which you absent-mindedly fiddle with. Does he say:
(a) I love you, warts and all?
(b) I'll dig it out with my Swiss Army knife?
(c) Nothing. He doesn't seem to notice?

3. You spent five hours getting ready but you still feel like a sockful of clothes pegs. Does he say:
(a) You look really gorgeous?
(b) You look like a sockful of clothes pegs?
(c) Nothing?

TEENAGE WORRIER'S FRIEND

4. The film starts and his head moves towards yours. What happens next:

(a) His lips find yours and he kisses you passionately awakening your Glands ... ?

(b) He says 'I wondered where that smell was coming from – have you been eating bacon crisps'?

(c) He moves his head back. He was trying to get a better view of the screen?

5. The film finishes and you turn to BYL – the film has stimulated you into philosophising on the Meaning of Life, the Universe and Everything. Does he:

(a) Listen intently to your Words of Wisdom?

(b) Tell you that your views might alter after reading Nietzsche and Plato?

(c) Look rather surprised and turn to his friend on his other side?

6. You are about to leave. What does BYL do:

(a) Walk you home with frequent stops to, ahem, rekindle your desires?

(b) Say goodbye, see you around?

(c) He's already gone?

why go to a film at all? Round the back of the Dustbins is good enuf for me...

Answers:

Mostly (a)s

You are V.V.V. lucky if this boy is the Object of Your Desires because you are in that enviable position of finding a BYL who also coincides with being a BLY. This is v.v.v. rare, although I can only really speak from the experience of two boyz. Brian liked me and though I do, of course, _like_ him, the magic is not there (and I can't help noticing his spots are). In contrast I fear I did not arouse Daniel's loins, though I do live in eternal hope.

Mostly (b)s

This boy doesn't really give the impression of being head over heels in lurve with you, but you never know. Lots of Boyz like to pretend they're not interested when in fact they are battling to maintain their cool, frightened and fighting against the disturbing passion that your presence arouses in them. Though it must be said that this probably isn't very likely.

Mostly (c)s

As you've never properly met this BYL it's a bit too early to say if he's in love with you though he probably isn't as he's unlikely to know who you are. Now is the time for getting to know him ie arranging convenient acts of feinting into his arms, falling off you bicycle so he picks you up Etck. But before you risk your life getting to speak to him, remember your lurve for him is probably based more on his outward appearance rather than anything truly deep and meaningful like the feeling that he's a kindred spirit and soul mate. Remember what Granny Chubb says: Never Judge A Book By It's Cover. (Especially this one heh heh).

TEENAGE WORRIER'S FRIEND

L.CHUBB'S MONTHLY GUIDE

JANUARY (To 19 Jan you're CAPRICORN
From 20th you're AQUARIUS)

SPECIAL DAZE: New Year's Day (always on Jan 1st, so V easy to remember). Off with Old, on with New Etck. Family is V.Sick with celebrating Dawn of New Era and the realisation that for them it'll be the same old sweat. Teenage Worrier's turn, tragically, but with the soft flutter of the Bluebird of Hope winging near, to their Diaries.

L. CHUBB's advice: Do Not resolve to keep a Diary (except this one of course), because recording your every quickening of the pulse can become a Pain, particularly if you don't have very many. This one can be filled in whenever you like. Any New Year Resolutions should be V Easy to keep so that a sense of buoyancy and achievement can be kept up until Mid Feb at least when Valentine's Day will make you forget NY Resolutions anyway. Here is a Sample List:

In 199_ I will:
1. Get up sometime each day, unless ill.
2. Get some sleep during the hours of darkness.
3. Wear clothes.
4. Eat something (in addition to fudge) each day.
FILL IN YOUR OWN HERE.

N.B. I am WORRIED I haven't put in Dates like CHINESE NEW YEAR (Feb) Etck. Maybe I will add them in the next edition.

IN SEASON: Sore, red hooters and peepers. Nose muffs and shades recommended.

PREDICTION: If you are a Capricorn, you will have had your birthday by Jan 20. If Aquarius, you will have it soon after. NB An astrologist once said he would give FREE Horoscopes to anyone who wrote in with their birth date and time etck, as long as they wrote back to say if the Horoscope was good. 92% of his clients responded saying he had sent them a V.Accurate record of themselves. And guess what? He had sent them all the same Horoscope! Not only that, but it was the star chart of a mass murderer. This has somewhat put me off Astrology (although it hasn't stopped me reading my Stars. Will we ever learn Etck Etck).

JAN WORRIES: How to be-a-better-person and make-this-year-better-than-last? Don't expect too much of yourself (see resolutions above). But always remember you are V.Privileged not to be in a War Zone or the person who had the idea for 'Eldorado' or shell suits (guilt, lash).

TEENAGE WORRIER'S FRIEND

FEBRUARY (Stars to 19th AQUARIUS from 20th PISCES)

SPESH DAY: Valentine's Day (Feb 14) see below.

Stay in bed for most of Feb as it is a V Gloomy month, esp Feb 14 which brings empty postbags to Teenage Worriers Worldwide.

NB If you MUST send a Valentine, send the L. CHUBB design below as a failure to respond will then not provoke disappointment.

outside ↘

Valentine!

Inside ↘

Er...... um..... I can't quite .....er.... make up my mind about you...

PREDICTION: Feb will only have 28 days in it unless it's a Leap Year (like 1996 will be). On Feb 29, Girlz can ask Boyz to marry them. They can ask them any other day too if they are really desperate, or their watch has stopped. If you were born on Feb 29 you are only about four years old and should not be reading this. Sadly, there is no Support Group for you, but comfort yourself with knowing how young you will be when the rest of us have reverted to weeing in the bed, shouting at lampposts, reading the Daily Telegraph or telling Teenage Worriers there's nothing to Worry about.

WEATHER Prediction: Weather V Dark. Sky on pavement.

FEB WORRIES: Existential wot-is-the-meaning-of-life type worries predominate during this time of year. Try to get out of yourself by taking long naps or time-travelling.

Moi & Rover failing to follow my Excellent advice for Feb...

TEENAGE WORRIER'S FRIEND

MARCH (To 21st PISCES From 22nd ARIES)

SPESH DAZE: MOTHER'S DAY (aaaaaah) on Mar 13 in 1994 and Mar 26 (1995).

Traditionally March 'Comes in like a lion and goes out like a lamb' which is supposed to mean that Winter changes to Spring about now. Despite Greenhouse effect, however, March is more likely to come in like a snail and exit like something out of Jurassic Park. That MARCH is an anagram of CHARM has little relation to its attributes unless you are V fond of gales. Teenage Worriers hate them because they play havoc with their dreads. Nonetheless, Brit Summer Time officially starts. In 1994 it will be on Mar 27.

At my ickle brother Benjy's school they don't make Mother's Day cards (because it is so V. Sad for ickle ones without mamas). This is true, but if you do have one, or someone else that you like known by the Caring Professions as a CARER, you may like to send her V soppy things and make her breakfast in bed (I did this literally last year as I tripped over our cat Rover while carrying the tray, and it's V.Hard to get runny egg off bri -nylon pillow cases).

Breakfast in Bed, L. Chubb-style

IN SEASON: Cold sores should be at their peak just now. Spots, plukes and zits will be sending forth spring shoots. Welcome Spring with dressing gown and two hot water botts.

PREDICTION: If a female over 15, you are likely to have a period this month. If a boy, visit a doctor should you experience these symptoms.

MARCH WORRIES: Flappy ears (producing Dumbo effect in high winds). I stick mine back with sticky tape.

sticky tape sales escalate in March

OUTSIDE↘

MUM!
Here, with all my Love, is a little FLOWER

INSIDE↘

SELF-RAISING FLOUR

Now..... will you bake me a cake?

Feminism's in Safe hands with L. Chubb's Mother's Day Card...

TEENAGE WORRIER'S FRIEND

APRIL (To 20th ARIES from 21st TAURUS)

SPESH DAZE: All Fool's Day (before noon on April 1). Easter (April 3 in 1994 and April 16 in 1995).

Ickle lambs and Easter chicks frolic in city farms. Ickle children see connection between cuddly baa lambs and ickle roast leg of same disguised with mint sauce, redcurrant jelly Etck (in houses where cooking still occurs) and become vegetarians. In the old daze, Granny Chubb says, people ate a lot of rabbit stew so she was V. Worried she had eaten the Easter Bunny. I am intending to become a vegetarian V.Soon.

Spring is now definitely here and the first snow of the year shld be decorating the apple blossom as you read this.

Teenage Worriers are allowed to recapture their lost Youth, (and if he has a friend, save him for me, ha ha) with painted eggs, eggy hunts Etck.

No one ever complains that the Christian Message has been drowned in a sea of Choccy, like they do at Christmas, but I am always V.Scared on Good Friday – especially if it goes dark at noon - why is it called 'Good' anyway? No wonder Jesus moved the stone and bunked off, he was thinking of his figure.

L. CHUBB'S APRIL FOOL TIP: Find a group of blokes digging up a road (in London it is V.Hard to find a road that is NOT being dug up, although it is still quite hard to find the blokes who are doing it) and tell them that a group of students disguised as police officers are arriving shortly to arrest them for an April Fool joke. Then hasten to your local Police Station and tell them that a group of students are digging up the road (for an April Fool joke). Stand back and watch the friendly and polite exchanges between the police officers and the road workers. Better still, choose a City Firm instead of road workers. Heh heh. Don't say you read it here though. OR Write to your MP saying 'All is discovered! Flee the country!' and see if he or she takes a holiday.

APRIL WORRIES: PEP (Post Easter Plumpness). Sprinkle branflakes on your choccy for extra fibre.

A Kindly Teenage Worrier comforts his sibling during a feast of Easter moderation....

TEENAGE WORRIER'S FRIEND

MAY (To 21st TAURUS ← My sign. Not that
(from 22nd GEMINI) I believe in it.
Ho Ho.

SPESH DAZE: MAYDAY (usually May 1st but May 2 in 1994). My B'day (May 2 every year - send me a card as I only got two last year and one was recycled - sob, wail, self pity, specially as there are four other people in my immediate family and two grannies, moan whinge Etck Etck).

'Ne'er cast a clout till May be out' says Granny Chubb. This does not mean you shouldn't deck anyone. It means keep on your vest, gloves, thermal underwear, hot water bottle-disguised-as-bumbag Etck. V.Good advice (although I draw the line at the bobble hat with Snoopy on that Granny Chubb knitted me last year. Does she have no idea of a Teenage Worrier's Dignity?).

Mayday is traditionally the day for dancing round phallic symbols (maypoles) and slinking provocatively into dark woods for dalliances Etck. Nowadays, you can only get darkness in the cinema or the laser shoot out arcade, neither of which is suitable for Dizzy Heights of Passion. If you were V.Good and V.Pretty you could get to be Queen of the May (pass the paper bag). Mayday was also the time when Workers marched together with banners, brass bands Etck to celebrate solidarity. Bring back solidarity! Bring back jobs! Or at least one job. For me. Pleeeeeeeese.

May Queen → (ho ho pull other one Etck)

HEALTH TIP: If you must have meringues, why not add low-cal mayonnaise?

MAY WORRIES: Rising sap, ickle buds Etck give rise to Major Willy Worries for Boyz (ie will it rise up and say hello to gorgeous pouting Michelle Unshockable from 5B and stay put whilst chatting politely about Religious Education to Aunt Jessica on the top deck of the number 37 bus?). Also glandular fever (can you get it from too much kissing? - chance wld be a fine thing I know but there are Teenage Worriers who have this prob. gnash). And Should-I-shave-my-legs-for-Summer-or-wait-till-it's-hot-enough-to-wear-a-swimsuit?

March of the Teenage Worriers....

BRING BACK MAYDAY

A WORRY SHARED IS A WORRY DOUBLED

Catz UNiON

WORRIERS OF THE WORLD UNITE

TEENAGE WORRIER'S FRIEND

JUNE (To 22nd, GEMINI / From 23rd, CANCER) { Lots of Teen Worriers are Nervous of being Cancer...

SPESH DAZE: Father's Day (June 19 in 1994, June 18 in 1995). The Longest Day (around June 21).

If you have a father, you can send him his own special card this month. Here are some L. CHUBB ideaz.

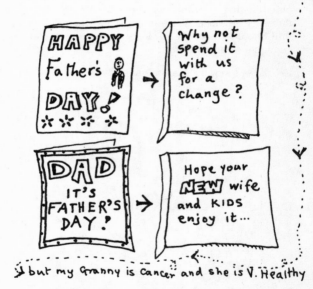

but my Granny is Cancer and she is V. Healthy

L O N G E S T D A Y: Wash face in dew first thing in morning. I know this means getting up early but it's worth it once a year to be beautiful forever.

Wimbledon Tennis starts in June which means Lesbians have a brief moment of high fashion. Sadly they are not quite so popular for the rest of the year, although my friend Hazel is doing her best to change this. Love all.

Gorgeous June is also the month for Gorgeous Exams and Gorgeous Glastonbury. But spare a thought for parents who may have their ickle darlings clamouring for sleeping bags, V.Expensive tickets Etck and failing to reach their Potential as they are too excited by the thought of Glasters to remember the Alphabet, never mind pass a Learned Exam.

CAMPAIGN to change EXAM dates so they do not collide with 1) Sunshine 2) Hay Fever 3) Anything else. On second thoughts, Campaign to stop exams as they are V.Unfair if you are feeling under-the-weather, a teensy bit poorly, etck etck.

IN SEASON: Ready-made salads are quickly available. I never eat fudge without one.

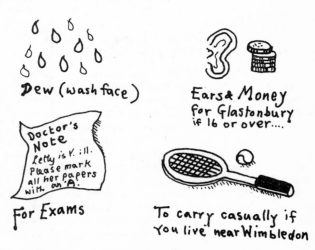

Dew (wash face)

Ears & Money for Glastonbury if 16 or over....

Doctor's Note
Letty is V. ill.
Please mark all her papers with an 'A'.

For Exams

To carry casually if you live near Wimbledon

Essentials for June...

TEENAGE WORRIER'S FRIEND

JULY (To 23rd CANCER from 24th LEO)

'In July the sun is hot, Is it shining? No it's not'. (Just to show the weather doesn't change here, these wise words were written by the songsmiths Flanders and Swann in about 1950, when the Hundred Years War had just ended.)

Wimbledon grinds to a close and the School Silly Season begins ie exams are over but you still have to turn up to twiddle your thumbs Etck. If you are at a posh fee-paying school you will get to start your holidays earlier than the rest of us and have more time to contemplate your navel languish over lurve Etck.

IN SEASON: Toffee is V.Fresh just now (not to be confused with health giving tofu) and can be eaten with watercress to reduce guilt factor. Strong mints taken with a slice of lemon are V Refreshing also.

JULY WORRIES: MONEY is V.Big Worry for Summer. When not at school (and soon it will be Hols hip hip yahooooo Etck) Teen Worriers find an overwhelming desire to spend dosh dough lolly Etck. But where to find it? Of course it wld be V.Nice if we could just curl up with a good friend (I mean book) and while away the time plaiting daisy chains and pondering The Meaning of Life Etck (as I do myself of course) but the need for Tender Young Plants such as ourselves to Explore the Great and Wonderful World and to attire ourselves in V.Nice clothes, go to see V.Improving films, get in lots of Videos (not that WE'VE GOT A VIDEO IN OUR HOUSE) Etck becomes somewhat Overwhelming. This leads to the heartbreaking Search for a Holiday job (it also leads to V. Nasty things like Theft Etck which I wld not recommend for fear of my book being Banned and my becoming V.Famous and having no Privacy from Sun reporters Etck). The govt has recently noticed that V.Poor people are more likely to steal things than V.Rich people but they are still letting poor people get poorer which seems V. Illogical to me. NB For those Teenage Worriers who are leaving school (yeeeech I wish I could stay on at V.Boring Sluggs Comp until I was 21, because however bad it is here, the Jobless Jungle seems even worse) then this is a V.V.V.V.Big Worry indeed.

JOIN THE L.CHUBB CAMPAIGN FOR JOB SWAPS. This means that adults with a full-time, fully-paid job (I know there are V.Few of them Etck Etck, but there are SOME) shld give one day a week of their job, plus half a day's pay, to the UNEMPLOYED, including Teenage Worriers everywhere. This wld give us all meaning, purpose, training Etck Etck. Also dosh. PLEEEEESE write to your MP on this one, marking your envelope (L.CHUBB JOBZ CAMPAIGN). See Form at end of book.

If your c.v. looks → like this, take advice.

Job apLiKAshuN

I wood Lik To HeLP iN a NEWz PAPeR BeKoz I do lik To riTe rubish V. V. V. MuTcH. TA.

TEENAGE WORRIER'S FRIEND

AUGUST (To 23rd **LEO** / From 24th **VIRGO**) ← From Lion to Virgin grr

Now the Summer Holidays beckon with open beaches, gleaming young bodies, the sounds of lazy guitars, surf plashing gently, cool drinks sipped through sugar encrusted straws, plagues of wasps, white paunches exploding out of unwisely chosen swimwear Etck. I must confess the range of holidays does serve to remind us of the injustices of life (Viz: I get a week in a Littlehampton B&B whereas Hazel swans off for a whole MONTH to Majorca where her parents' friends have a bijou villa complete with swimming pool and sound effects as above). Aggy, however, hasn't been out of London for ten years except for a weekend in Birmingham, so I shouldn't complain (but I will anyway, moan gnash).

Since Aug is a time when you hope for a Holiday Romance (even if the only Italians you can meet are the waiters at the Pizza-Shack who got their accents off Cornetto ads), it is not the time to consider a major Hair Re-style unless you are staying in a wilderness with your Granny and therefore only she will care what you look like. On le autre main - as they say in France, where the V.Handsome Daniel goes each year gnash swoooon Etck - it cld be worse being nagged by your Gran than by anyone else. Ie 'Pink will be a good colour for hair, when brunette is a good colour for Begonias' OR 'in MY day, we took the combs OUT of our hair after using them.' OR 'You seem to have got a NECKLACE tangled in your hair darling, let me see if I can YANK it out' Etck Etck. In fact, no time is the right time for a major hair re-style in my opinion and I am keeping my wholewheat spaghetti ratstails as long as I can, espesh since when I cut them my head seemed but a distant dot on the horizon.

But I digress.

SUMMER and all year TIP: Always carry several condoms just in case (chance wld be a fine thing I know and anyway now that I'm definitely going to be a nun I don't see much point in carrying one, or even carrying on ...) and always remember to use a V.Good NON-OILY spermicide, too. Always always use water based creams Etck as oily ones can damage condoms and you don't want to hear the patter of incy feet just yet, do you? Or worse by far, catch AIDS. One mistake is enough, as my big brother's friend tragically discovered.

L. CHUBB PREDICTION: Aug will have 31 days in it. You will fall in Lurve. Your Lurve may be returned in which case you will experience Perfect BLISS. Bliss, as you may have heard, tends to make up for in height what it lacks in length Etck Etck but we must remain eternally hopeful amid the Worries. If by any chance your Lurve does not work out it is worth noticing that TEEN WORRIERS inevitably fall in Lurve in Aug so you are bound to fall in Lurve again next Aug (or even at Christmas which is the next most popular nooky season).

AUG WORRIES: Red hooters are back, only this time it's caused by Sun minus Ozone. To go brown or not? Why frazzle yourself to a crisp when you can get V.Good fake tans that cost £80 zillion and leave you with V.Pleasant Zebra effect? Since sun creams also cost £80 zillion I prefer the Pale-and-Interesting look. This is naturally easier to achieve if you are a pinky white person in the first place.

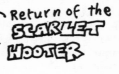

Return of the SCARLET HOOTER

SEPTEMBER (To 23rd VIRGO From 24th LIBRA)

Back to school (arg yeeech) with no summer to look forward to yearningly, and only a V.Disappointing one to look back on yearningly. When you come back for the autumn term, School is divided into those whose summer holidays were a Cheap Day Return to Frinton (worth it, however, for the graffiti saying 'Harwich For The Continent, Frinton For The Incontinent ha-ha, yeech) or a Day At The Zoo watching monkeys play Doctors and Nurses, and the Spoiled Little Rich Kids who come back from Tenerife looking like teenagers from Dynasty, if there was anyone young enough not to need their own personal plastic surgeon in Dynasty. This division is what you call Them and Us. It can take till Christmas to Heal The Wounds caused by such injustice, and sometimes longer than that, like a Lifetime. Etck.

If you have left school you are now going into Further Education (which means taking out National Debt-style loans so that you can afford running water and a packet of crisps twice a week). OR, you are now going to Job Centres or Yoof Unemployment Schemes, Cardboard boxes Etck. If you have a job, pleeeeeeeese write and tell me how you got it. I hope V.Much that they will take me on a Nun-employment scheme - all I ask is a dry cell of my own that's fit for Human Habitation, ha-ha, geddit.

L.CHUBB TIP: Brighten up your Winter Wardrobe with a new coat (of paint ho ho. Try it on your clothes, too). I have heard of people who multiply their shoes by painting them different colours on different days, but personally I reckon the whole question of clothes is just another Conspiracy Against Worriers. I don't see why everybody shouldn't wear the same smock. People say it's Sexless, but I reckon it just increases your Curiosity about just how different from you the other person is Underneath. In the case of Daniel and Me, I imagine it's considerable (pant, pant, phew!). In the case of Hazel and Me it's considerable too (grrr, boo-hoo, Unfair Etck).

SEPT WORRIES: New School Year, wot will teechers be like? Etck. Freckles fade, but Cold sores re-emerge (every silver lining has a cloud Etck). Flavour your fudge with the last of the garden's fresh herbs (wot garden? OK, window box, if you're lucky enough to have a window).

Wot might have been (sigh). The three "S"s of Summer. THOUGHT: why do people hisssss at BAD things? Anyway, now it's Sept. Boo Hoo Whinge Etck.

TEENAGE WORRIER'S FRIEND

OCTOBER (To 23rd LIBRA From 24th SCORPIO)

SPESH DAZE: Summer Officially Ends (boo hoo yearn) on Oct 23 in 1994 and Oct 29 in 1995. Just as well they have dates for it, because you wouldn't be able to tell otherwise. Hallowe'en is always on Oct 31, when ghoulies ghosties long legged beasties Etck tramp about to scare superstitious Teenage Worriers. What a farce Etck. There are no Worries as Scary as the ones you invent for yourself, and I know many Worriers who would rather spend just a quiet hour or two with a Ghoulie or Ghostie discussing such matters as the After Banana Experience than with any of the ones that pop out of the Abyss Of The Soul looking like your Dad and wielding a hedgetrimmer. L.CHUBB motto: grab a Ghoulie by the Goolies just to show you're friendly. *Not recommended if the Ghoulie is bigger than you*

Autumn leaves drift by your window and you are filled with N O S T A L G I A for Summer. The pimply gigolo (or gigolette) you met on Brighton pier and who never replied to your 15 postcards suddenly seems like a Greek God(dess). Why did you complain of sunburn Etck in those Halcyon days when the sky was always blue? And now it's OVER it's OVER ... blah blah violins, lost hope Etck. Try to bear in mind that Summer will be back eventually after the Long Dark Night of British Winter Etck. In fact, if Greenhouse Effect Panic is all true, in the end it may never go away again, and cause agonising Divided Loyalty condition. *13 Thirteen*

I have written '13' lots of times to overcome my WORRY

Hallowe'en remains a nightmare (or nitmare, if the head lice at my baby brother's Infants school continue to plague me as they have all Summer) for Superstitious Teen Worriers. But take heart! The Coat of Arms of the USA includes 13 stars, 13 stripes, 13 arrows in the Eagle's talon and 13 letters in the Motto. Look where it got them! (Aaargh, yeech, on second thoughts...). Nonetheless, Hallowe'en is V.Good excuse for having a party. (Ask everyone to dress up). This will ensure much recycling of bin bags goes on, which is Ecologically Sound. Also, YOU can dress up as Spanish Dancer and therefore upstage everyone else (who will have loominous green fangs Etck) and waltz off into Moonset with Mysterious, tall dark Dracula.

HALLOWE'EN TIP: Find pumpkin. Get four white mice, a couple of lizards, Fairy Godmother, wand Etck. OR look at Charles and Diana and Think Again.

OCTOBER WORRIES: As the year draws to a close, Teenage Worriers wonder, Have they grown enough? Or too much? Have they stopped altogether? Or shot up? Etck.

L. CHUBB'S GROWING TIPS: Boyz! Wear a Top Hat! Add inches! Join the nobs! They are getting V.Much richer while the poor are wasting away anyway, so why not join the winning side which is wot the Govt think we can all do if we try V.Hard and have no scruples Etck moan. Alternatively, if too tall, stoop. It works for me.

THE 8 HOUR PUMPKIN

I spent 4 hours cutting this pumpkin for my ickle brother BENJY. When he saw it he burst into tears of joy and hid under his bed for the next 4 hours...

NOVEMBER (To 22nd SCORPIO
From 23rd SAGITTARIUS)

F
O
G

D
A
M
P

L
E
A
V
E
S

E
T
C
K

SPESH DAZE: BONFIRE NIGHT (Nov 5th every year),
Remembrance Sunday (Nov 13 in 1994, Nov 12 in 1995)
when we all remember the soldiers who died in two world
wars and everyone who wants to look a Good Person wears
a Red Poppy on the telly (even the ones who spend the
rest of the year flogging weapons to governments run by
loony soldiers in rakish berets Etck Etck). I always lose my
Poppies and end up buying five red and five white (the
Pacifist version) as I feel so wracked with guilt if I don't
have one on which shows I am as good as all those
politicians, newscasters, pundits Etck.

'No birds No bees No flowers No trees No health No ease
November.'

Ye poet Thomas Hood wrote something like that many
years ago which only goes to show that November has
been here before. I must confess I have a sneaky liking for
the fog, damp leaves, conkers Etck. It is V.Nice to sit by an
open fire roasting marshmallows even if your fire is a one
bar electric since the radiators always sound like Granny
Chubb's tummy rumbling in our house, but never give out
any heat (I know we're lucky to HAVE radiators, but it
would be V.Nice to have one working for some of the
winter because I am V.Fed up having nowhere to dry my
socks).

November is V.Good for hypochondriacs (a sin of which,
as you know, I am NOT guilty, at least not more than three
or four times a day) as you will generally have V.Bad colds
and flu and it is a reason to snuggle up with 50 blankets
and a hot water bottle at each corner and not go out (not
because you've nowhere to go to, of course, but out of
CHOICE ahem).

I used to be V.Scared of Firework night because my Big
Brother used to put bangers in apples Etck but those days

are gone and now no-one lights blue touch paper and runs like hell except the Municipal Display makers, who spend 50 zillion quid on ten minutes puffs and pops. Still, it brings the community together Etck, and makes them realise there is more to life than just seeing money go up in smoke (I mean waiting for their meals-on-wheels, Social Insecurity Money Etck).

And what is Life if we cannot have Bread and Circuses Etck? Bonfire Displays are also V.Good for nooky as you casn get lost in dark with your Object of Desire and many a Lurve has been ignited along with a sparkler, though there is a risk that the extra firepower of the Sensational Finale may suddenly illuminate your attempts to read the label on your partner's underwear and cause Embarrassment. Swooon.

NOVEMBER WORRIES: Cold sores are getting up a good scab now for the party season. Just when you've zapped one, another appears. Hay fever shld be over except in V.Rare cases. If you experience these symptoms now you may just be V.Allergic. Try getting rid of all the things you like, and see if it stops.

L. CHUBB TIPS: Brighten up lank winter locks with a number one haircut. Wear woolly hats after. Always wear something to cover your top bits and your bottom bits as it is likely to be cold. Hand covers useful if you MUST go out. After covering your jacket potato with lashings of cream, butter and fatty cheeses, sprinkles on a smidgeon of grated parsley. Ensure your Hot Chocolate is low-alcohol.

DECEMBER (To 22nd SAGITTARIUS)
(From 23rd CAPRICORN)

SPESH DAZE: Dec 22, shortest day (ie darkest bleakest least hours gloom Etck Etck). CHRISTMAS DAY (Hohoho definitely on Dec 25). Also Christmas Eve (always on Dec 24), Boxing Day always on Dec 26 (and not about thumping people, but about taking them presents in boxes, not a lot of people Know That) and NEW YEAR'S EVE (always on Dec 31, see also JAN, above, for after effects and sense of life coming full circle Etck).

As the chill descends, the daze draw in, the nights (passionless as ever) grow longer and Teenage Worriers slink slowly into the Slough of Despond. Then, whap, zammy in comes the Festive Season (which actually started two months ago as Moaning Minnies and Cheerless Charlies are always telling us). It is a great thing that Christmas comes in the middle of Winter because otherwise what wld we have to moan about except gloom, cold Etck Etck. Also it fills you with hope that you might get something you like or better still meet something you like under mistletoe at all the V.Exciting rave-ups to which you are bound to be invited.

Ho
Ho
Ho!

But, amid the carolling carols Etck spare a thought for the Teenage Worrier whose Birthday falls on this Day. She or He will never have had a proper B'day all of their own and therefore, all their lives, they will have had fewer presents. By the age of 15, this can lead to a warped personality without careful nurturing and alas, there is no support group for these tortured individuals.

DECEMBER WORRIES: Money. Always pressing but V.Bad just now as essential to buy one or two prezzies. Last year Hazel gave me a book which had on the flyleaf 'Darling Hazel, all our love on your ninth birthday, Mama'. This seemed to me a double insult, although I am V. in favour of recycling generally and presents in particular. Particularly, f'rinstance, last year's muffler from Granny Chubb, the unopened fountain pen italic handwriting set from Granny Gosling, the two marbles and a biro from my baby brother Benjy Etck, but I can't think who to give them to. WHETHER TO HANG MISTLETOE: Worth it, even if nobody nice drops by. You never know.

Acne, AIDS, Agony Aunts, Baldness, Boyz, Bras, Books, Cleavage, Cosmetics arg. All the Worries that I outlined in my modest Alphabet 'I WAS A TEENAGE WORRIER' (on sale at all good bookshops Etck) come crowding in on me once more as the Year hurtles to a close. Have I Saved the Planet? Stopped Worrying? Started Living? Made any Dosh? Become a Nun? Had Sex? Gone to a New Year's Eve Party? Will I be a better person Next Year? What will it bring? Yeeeech, bury head in snow if there was any grrrr, moan Etck.

L. CHUBB TIP: Turn to Jan and begin again, aware of life's pageant Etck. OR Go to bed with Rover (my cat) and sneeze the night away.

My ickle bruvver pondering the true spirit of ChristMas with his ickle pals.

TEENAGE WORRIER'S FRIEND

MONTH: July   YEAR 199_5

school grue (unless it's hols ho ho

Moanday ___

It is school holidays. I might sleep in Sian's tent tonight. My Dad thinks I am incapable.

Chewsday ___ START THIS DIARY where you want. Could Be SPRING!

Wensdy ___

Thirsty ___ Measure Nose and other WORRYING BITS.

Frydy ___

SATdownallday ___ ☼ ♡♡ First weekend in Diary.

FUNday (we hope) ___

MONTH: _Fill in_   YEAR 199_
←   _month, year_ →
_____
Moanday __ ←   _and date_

_____
Chewsday __   You will feel V. Happy today for No reason.

♡ ❤
♡♡
_____
Wensdy __
❤

♡
_____
Thirsty __

_____
Frydy __   If this is a Friday 13ᵗʰ DO NOT
~~WORRY~~ - see NOTES for OCTOBER

_____
SATdownallday __   2nd weekend in Diary

_____
FUNday (we hope) __

TEENAGE WORRIER'S FRIEND

MONTH: _____   YEAR 199_

FOOD WEEK

Cottage
Loaf
↓

Moanday __ Why not bake your own bread? v. Useful as a Door stop.

Chewsday __ Alternatively, take TOAST & scrape it.

Wensdy __ Remember to have some food every day!

Thirsty __ Why stop at Toffee? Add Fudge, choccy, caramel and a slice of Lemon.

Frydy __ Fry bananas for your family.

SATdownallday __ **WEEKEND!**

FUNday (we hope) __ Cooking is FUN! So open that packet of OVEN CHIPS now.

MONTH: **FOOD SECTION**   YEAR 199_

Moanday __   Remember to get dressed.

Chewsday __   Try eating old fashioned-
Style with a knife, fork and plate. At a
TABLE.

Wensdy __ How about RED food today? A good
balanced meal wld be baked beans, smarties
& a tomato.

Thirsty __   THIRSTY? Drink lo-cal water.

Frydy __ Cook for ENTIRE household.

SATdownallday __ Throw up over entire
household.

FUNday (we hope) __ Call Docter.

TEENAGE WORRIER'S FRIEND

MONTH: _____   YEAR 199_

Moanday ___ **CONGRATULATIONS!** You have
Kept this Diary for FOUR WEEKS!

Chewsday ___

Wensdy ___

Thirsty ___

Frydy ___ Have You been to the DENTIST this year?

SATdownallday ___ Wash face if you have not
done so this year.

FUNday (we hope) ___

DIARY

MONTH: YEAR 199_

Moanday ___

Chewsday ___   Worry, worry, worry.

Wensdy ___   Hare you written to your granny?

Thirsty ___

Frydy ___   Did you feed the cat? Goldfish? Etck.

SATdownallday ___

FUNday (we hope) ___

TEENAGE WORRIER'S FRIEND

MONTH: YEAR 199_

Moanday __ ARG! Did you forget somebody's BIRTHDAY?

Chewsday __ Write to PM about HORRIBLE WORLD.

Wensdy __

Thirsty __

Frydy __ Get in big FUDGE supply.

SATdownallday __
LOAF
and the world
LOAFS with
You

FUNday (we hope) __

DIARY

MONTH: _____   YEAR 199_

Moanday __ Write to MP about longer School
Holidays, Summer, Hair, World Peace Etck.

Chewsday __ BUY SPOT CREAM + BOOK on ACNE

WOT'S
THIS?
↓

Wensdy __ ☼ INVASION of the PLUKES

Thirsty __ Have you cleaned your teeth this week?

Frydy __ Wash 14 socks — all of them odd.

SATdownallday __ Buy MORE SPOT CREAM

FUNday (we hope) __ call Doctor re-spots

MONTH: *MUSIC FORTNIGHT* YEAR 199_

Moanday ___ "IF Music be the food of LURVE, Play on" — W. Shakespeare.

Chewsday ___ PRACTISE your PIANO, recorder, guitar, comb & paper Etck.

V. Successful SONG LYRIC (anyone can do it...)

Wensdy ___ Do - be - doo - be .. doo ... wop.

Thirsty ___

Frydy ___ COMPOSE Hit Song today.

SATdownallday ___ As above.

FUNday (we hope) ___

MONTH: MUSIC Fortnight YEAR 199_

_____

Moanday __ Get agent for Hit Song.

_____

Chewsday __

_____

Wensdy __ Remember to have BATH - and sing in it.

_____

Thirsty __ SLOg-a-log-a-loog-a-log-a-loo ←······

bam-boony.

V. good chorus

_____

Frydy __

Go to CLUB

_____

SATdownallday __

_____

FUNday (we hope) __ Call Doc re-deafness.

TEENAGE WORRIER'S FRIEND

MONTH: YEAR 199_

Moanday __

Chewsday __

Wensdy __   Did you Forget to fill in last week?

Thirsty __

Frydy __ Have little WORRY about Life's Rich Tapestry.

SATdownallday __ Have you written to your Aunt?

FUNday (we hope) __

MONTH: YEAR 199_

Moanday __   Get NIT shampoo - Just in case.

Chewsday __

Wensdy __   And flea powder

Thirsty __

Frydy __

SATdownallday __   Write to your true LURVE ♥♥

FUNday (we hope) __

TEENAGE WORRIER'S FRIEND

MONTH: YEAR 199_

Moanday __   L. Chubb Prediction: It will rain sometime this week.....

Chewsday __

Wensdy __   Disinfect sock drawer B4 they walk off by themselves.

Thirsty __

Frydy __

SATdownallday __   ☀

FUNday (we hope) __

DIARY

MONTH: YEAR 199_

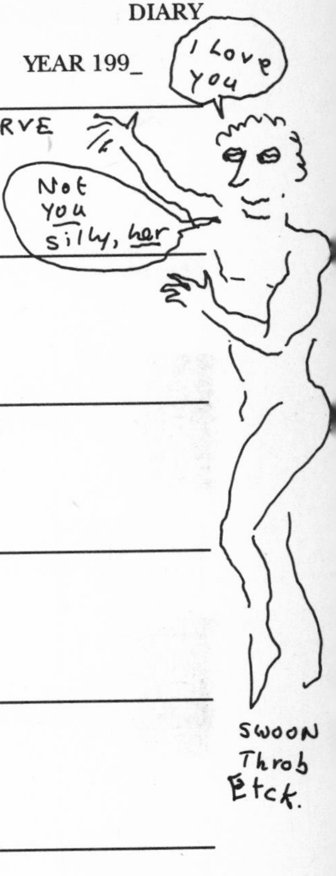

Moanday __ Speak to TRUE LURVE on telephone.

Chewsday __ CRY.

Wensdy __ Feel a bit better.

Thirsty __ Pine.

Frydy __ Take a cold shower.

SATdownallday __

FUNday (we hope) __

TEENAGE WORRIER'S FRIEND

MONTH: *Lazy week*   YEAR 199_

Moanday __   Take it EASY (unless doing Exams Eee

Chewsday __   A Woman's right to SNOOZE.

Wensdy __   Have little nap

Thirsty __   Have little cat-nap

Frydy __   Get up v. slowly.

SATdownallday __ SAT in bed all day

FUNday (we hope) __ 3 meals in Bed.

MONTH: *Lazy week 2* YEAR 199_

Moanday __ Exercise eyelids by gently opening eyes once or twice.

Chewsday __ Z Z Z Z Z Z Z Z Z Z · · · · · · · · · · ·

Wensdy __ Z Z Z Z Z Z · · · · · · · ? · · · ·

Thirsty __ Oh well · · · if you've had a busy week I'm SORRY.

Frydy __ You can alway have a lazy week NEXT week · · · ·

SATdownallday __ GUILT, GUILT.

FUNday (we hope) __ Z Z Z Z Z Z Z Z Z Z Z

TEENAGE WORRIER'S FRIEND

MONTH: _____   YEAR 199_

Moanday __ COR! Are you really still filling
this in? V.V. Good!

Play NOUGHTS
& CROSSES
here ↓

Chewsday __

Wensdy __

Thirsty __

Frydy __

SATdownallday __

FUNday (we hope) __

MONTH: V. Boring Week. YEAR 199_

Moanday __

watch T.V.

Chewsday __

Watch T.V.

Wensdy __

Watch T.V.

Thirsty __

Watch T.V.

Frydy __

If you don't have a T.V. watch the goldfish.

SATdownallday __

If you don't have a goldfish go to Laundnrette.

FUNday (we hope) __

watch washing spinning round.

TEENAGE WORRIER'S FRIEND

MONTH: YEAR 199_

Moanday — **HYGIENE** week!

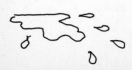

Chewsday — Floss teeth

Wensdy — Remove furry green jackets from cups

Thirsty — Look under your BED.

Frydy — Disinfect sock drawer (again). Also places where socks have been.

SATdownallday — Have little WORRY about GERMS.

FUNday (we hope) — Clean mirror. Feel sad at your reflection, since you can now see your ZITS.

DIARY

MONTH: _____ YEAR 199_

Moanday — **HYGIENE** week 2!

Chewsday __ See how many dried up felt tip pens
you can find

Wensdy __ OPEN BEDROOM WINDOW! RADICAL!

Thirsty __ OK ... you've looked ... but do you
dare to go ... under ... the BED.

Frydy __ List what you found under bed. V.
Interesting for yr. grandchildren ...

SATdownallday __ Fold some clothes.

FUNday (we hope) __ Remove some grafitti from
your wall.

P
I
N
G

P
O
N
G

TEENAGE WORRIER'S FRIEND

MONTH: YEAR 199_

Moanday ___ Health Fortnight!

Chewsday ___ Get Dictionary of Symptoms from LIBRARY & have little worry.

Wensdy ___ Make appts with Doc, Dentist, Alt Health people Etck.

Thirsty ___ Take pulse. Have little worry.

Frydy ___ Check temperature. Have little worry.

SATdownallday ___ Check pulses of Loved Ones.

FUNday (we hope) ___

← Dust mites are everywhere. SNEEZE.

DIARY

MONTH: YEAR 199_

Moanday __ Eat lots of Fruit and neg with all your sweeties.

❄

Chewsday __ check for NITS (again) and Varoukas.

Wensdy __ Why won't the Doc give me an X-ray, Brain Scan Etck.? Unfair. Sob.

❄

Thirsty __ Drink lots of FILTERED water with your FIZZY POP.

❄
❄

Frydy __ ExERCISE regularly by walking   ❄ ❄
across playground, bathroom, Etck.

❄ ❄

SATdownallday __ Swap Dic. of Symptoms for MEDICAL ENCYCLOPAEDIA. (If Library open. Hah!)

FUNday (we hope) __ Check to see 999 no. is working.

TEENAGE WORRIER'S FRIEND

MONTH: YEAR 199_

Moanday __

Chewsday __

Wensdy __

Thirsty __

Frydy __   Arg! Forgot to get up.

SATdownallday __

FUNday (we hope) __

MONTH: Another V. BORING YEAR 199_
WEEK.

Moanday ___ Washed hair

Chewsday ___ Telephone call. Wrong number.

Wensdy ___ Talked to some people.

Thirsty ___ Watched some T.V.

Frydy ___ Watched some more T.V.

SATdownallday ___ Slept all day.

FUNday (we hope) ___ Watched T.V.

TEENAGE WORRIER'S FRIEND

MONTH: Art week 1   YEAR 199_

Moanday __ Paint ickle picture in watercolours.

Chewsday __ Get ickle sibling to paint ickle picture (aaaah...)

Wensdy __ Take ickle sibling's picture to POSH GALLERY and say it is work of 95 yr old MINER.

Thirsty __ spend dosh from posh gallery on lots of v. nice CLOTHES, I mean PAINTS.

Frydy __ PAINT BIG MURAL on front of house (if in flat, get scaffolding).

SATdownallday __ Sell Mural.

FUNday (we hope) __ Move out of house & live in caravan.

MONTH: Art Week 2 YEAR 199_

Moanday — Save milk bottle tops for collage.

Chewsday — Save loo rolls for hamster.

Wensdy — Draw pic of world covered in pink satin.

Thirsty — Dance in paint.

Frydy — Decorate Hall of School with bin bags and Drinks cans as a STATEMENT.

SATdownallday — write to PM demanding more bigger ART.

FUNday (we hope) —

More Bigger ART NOW

TEENAGE WORRIER'S FRIEND

MONTH: _____ YEAR 199_

Moanday __

Chewsday __

Wensdy __ About this time of year I clear out all my old toys...

Thirsty __ And decide to keep them...

Frydy __ Till next year...

SATdownallday __

FUNday (we hope) __

MONTH: YEAR 199_

Moanday __ If you are still keeping this diary you win the LETTY CHUBB Longevity Award.

Chewsday __

Wensdy __

Thirsty __

Frydy __

SATdownallday __

FUNday (we hope) __ Have Teddy Bears Picnic to recapture LOST YOO F.

TEENAGE WORRIER'S FRIEND

MONTH: YEAR 199_

Moanday __ Fill in the Last few days of
this DIARY.

Nice

Chewsday __

NICE

Wensdy __ Today I am going to be v. Nice.

Nice

Nice

Thirsty __ I am going to be v. Nice Today.

Nice

Frydy __ I will be v. nice next week, as this
week I have P.M.T.

SATdownallday __

Nice

FUNday (we hope) __

MONTH: YEAR 199_

Moanday — **WEEK** for Being **NICE**

Chewsday __ ☺

Wensdy __ ☺

Thirsty ⋅ ☺

Frydy __ ☺

SATdownallday __   Oh well... try again ☹
next year

FUNday (we hope) __ Cheat. It's easy to be ☺
nice on FuNday.

TEENAGE WORRIER'S FRIEND

MONTH: (☺) (☺) YEAR 199_

IF
RGAD
IN
RHYTHM
THIS
LITTLE
DITTY
WILL
CHEER
YOU
IN
THE
MIDST
OF
GLOOM
DESPONDENCY
DOOM
SADNESS
MISERY
PESSIMISM
BLEAKNESS
DESPAIR
DESPONDENCY
PIQUE
APATHY
SLOTH
SORROW
NIHILISM
DEFEAT

Moanday — Dum-di-dum-di-dum.

Chewsday — diddle-e...diddle-di...do

Wensdy — tumpty tumpty tum

Thirsty — piddly piddly poo.

Frydy — Bingly bingly bingle

SATdownallday — Wingly wongly wung

FUNday (we hope) — Fiddely fiddely Fido

DIARY

MONTH: (◡̈) (◡̈)   YEAR 199_

ANXIETY

Moanday — Bingly Bongly Bun.

MISGIVING
MELANCHOLY
INFELICITY
DEJECTION
DEPRESSION

Chewsday — Taraddidle!

LOWNESS
OPPRESSION
MOPINESS
GLUMNESS
GRIEF

Wensdy — Taradiddle!

SORROW
ETCK.
ETCK.
Arggh!
After

Thirsty — Clumpety clumpetty

writing
all that
I think
I had
better

Frydy — Clump!

hum
this
ickle
DITTY.
Then

SATdownallday — Bing Bong Bing Bong

I will
feel
JOY
PLEASURE
PEACE

FUNday (we hope) — Bing Bong Bump.

ETCK
ETCK.

TEENAGE WORRIER'S FRIEND

MONTH: _____   YEAR 199_

Moanday — Hi! It's a NEW WEEK!

Chewsday — Gosh! Tuesday again!

Wensdy — Wednesday - whoopee!

Thirsty — Hurrah for Gorgeous Thursday!

Frydy — Fabulous Friday!

SATdownallday — WEEKEND!

FUNday (we hope) — My cup overfloweth!

MONTH: ❀ ❀   YEAR 199_ ♫

Moanday — I'm as happy as a lark!
❀
The bluebird
of
Happiness →

Chewsday — As bright as a button!
♫

❀ ❀

Wensdy — As merry as a trivet !

Thirsty — Beg one Dull Care!

Frydy — Worry worry worry worry.

SATdownallday — The Ditty on pages 76 & 77
definitely works...

FUNday (we hope) — ... For a few days.

TEENAGE WORRIER'S FRIEND

MONTH: YEAR 199_

Moanday ___

Chewsday ___

Wensdy ___

Thirsty ___

Frydy ___

SATdownallday ___

FUNday (we hope) ___

MONTH: YEAR 199_

Moanday __

Chewsday __

Wensdy __

Thirsty __

Frydy __

SATdownallday __

FUNday (we hope) __

MONTH: ____   YEAR 199_

Moanday __ Did you miss me not writing on the last 2 pages?

Chewsday __ How are you in YOURSELF?

Wensdy __ Sorry. I was TIRED

Thirsty __ I DO care. I really do

Frydy __

Get in BIG CHOCCY SUPPLY.

SATdownallday __

FUNday (we hope) __

DIARY

MONTH: YEAR 199_

Moanday __ What do YOU MEAN, YOU won't be my FRIEND any more?

Chewsday __

Wensdy __ NOBODY CARES

Thirsty __

Frydy __  Every silver lining has a cloud

SATdownallday __

FUNday (we hope) __

TEENAGE WORRIER'S FRIEND

Moanday — FRIENDS week.

Chewsday — If you stole your best friend's boyfriend - give him back.

Wensdy — Why not write Everyone's Birthday in your DIARY? So you can forget them (he he)

Thirsty — How about making a new friend today?

Frydy — Here is my new friend. He is called Basil

SATdownallday — Basil has left me for a SPIDER!

FUNday (we hope) — Nobody cares.

MONTH: YEAR 199_   H¡

Moanday —   FRIENDS Week 2.

Chewsday __ If at first you don't succeed...

Wensdy __ Fry fry fry again. Get sunburnt with
a friend.

Thirsty __ Buy your best FRIEND a DRESS.

Frydy __ Basil didn't like the Dress.

SATdownallday __ Nobody cares.

FUNday (we hope) __ Nobody at all.

TEENAGE WORRIER'S FRIEND

MONTH: YEAR 199_

Moanday __ BE USEFUL week.

Chewsday __ Cook someone for breakfast.
I mean cook breakfast for someone.

Wensdy __ Er... hoover room sometime.

Thirsty __ Hoover room sometime.

Frydy __ Take hoover to menders.

SATdownallday __ Lick floor clean.

FUNday (we hope) __ Call Doctor

(left margin, vertical) KINDNESS COSTS A LOT

DIARY

MONTH: _____   YEAR 199_

Moanday __   TRY TO BE USEFUL AGAIN

Chewsday __   Make bed.

Wensdy __ Sleep in old bed as one I made not V. Comfy.

Thirsty __ Do shopping.

Frydy __ Return smoked salmon & asparagus to supermarket in exchange for two TRolleys of Groceries.

SATdownallday __ Look after Baby Brother ALL DAY.

FUNday (we hope) __ Call Doctor.

FINE WORDS BUTTER NO PARSNIPS

MONTH: YEAR 199_

L
C
H
U
B
B'S

D
I
C
T
I
O
N
A
R
Y

Moanday __ This week I have decided to invent a new word each day.

Chewsday __ VOM: a colour between violet and indigo.

Wensdy __ BLUKE: v. big pustule.

Thirsty __ SNERK: v. creepy individual.

Frydy __ PLASHIOUS: v.v. sexy yet, um, ethereal at the same time. SWOON.

SATdownallday __ SNOD: Fluff in pockets, bags Etck.

FUNday (we hope) __ GLEMINATE: To stare at ceiling for long periods.

DIARY

MONTH: _____ YEAR 199_

Moanday __ Yes! I'll invent a few more.

Chewsday __ QUERVE: snake-hipped male.
(swoon)

Wensdy __ GLUMMENSCHMERZ: V.V. Anxious
person.

Thirsty __ Oh well. You try it ....

Frydy __

SATdownallday __ Sticks and Stones may break my
bones ...

FUNday (we hope) __ but words will ALWAYS
hurt me

TEENAGE WORRIER'S FRIEND

MONTH: YEAR 199_

Moanday __ Have you ever thought that all
the books in the English language contain
only 26 LETTERS?!

Chewsday __

Wensdy __

Thirsty __ Fall in Love. Now.

Frydy __

SATdownallday __

FUNday (we hope) __

DIARY

MONTH: YEAR 199_

Moanday __

Chewsday __

Wensdy __

Thirsty __

Frydy __

Stay in Love if poss.

SATdownallday __

FUNday (we hope) __   call psychiatrist.

Moanday — ECOLOGY TIME

Chewsday — Save paper. Tippex out this Diary and use again next year.

Wensdy — Why not take a WALK to school. Even if it IS five minutes.

Thirsty — Write to PM about HORRIBLE motorways.

Frydy — Write to MP about V. Nice Trains. e.g. DO NOT PRIVATISE.

SATdownallday — Feel guilty about writing letters, so re-use stamps.

FUNday (we hope) — Plant a tree.

MONTH: YEAR 199_

Moanday __ Write to Newspapers suggesting they get SMALLER. Suggest 'The SUN' disappears alto getter.

Chewsday __ Do not use hairsprays Etck more than once a day.

Wensdy __ Feel v. Gnilty about plastic.

Thirsty __ Notice how much plastic is in world.

Frydy __ Worry about fate of planet.

SATdownallday __ Retire to bed.

FUNday (we hope) __ Call Doctor.

MONTH: _____   YEAR 199_

_____

Moanday ___

Thought
I'd leave
these
blank   _____
as you   Chewsday ___
may
want to
pack
a LOT
of   _____
words   Wensdy ___
in this
week.
I don't   _____
know   Thirsty ___
why,
it's
just
a feeling _____
I have.   Frydy ___
Actually
I wish
I'd made
this   _____
this   SATdownallday ___
Diary
BIGGER
cos
the   _____
the   FUNday (we hope) ___
you
could

DIARY

MONTH: YEAR 199_

Moanday ___

> have
> written
> mone
> and then

Chewsday ___

> You
> might
> have got
> Your

Wensdy ___

> diary
> PUBLISHED
> and
> made
> lots of

Thirsty ___

> DOSH
> LOOT
> MONEY
> LUCRE

Frydy ___

> DOUGH
> LOLLY
> GOLD
> ETCK.

SATdownallday ___

> ETCk.

FUNday (we hope) ___

TEENAGE WORRIER'S FRIEND

MONTH: _____ YEAR 199_

Moanday ___ Oh this Diary is nearing
its end

Chewsday ___ Goodbye farewell oh
Teenage Friend.

Wensdy ___ Wash hair if you haven't
done so already this year.

Thirsty ___ Cut toe and fingernails too.

(Etck)

Frydy ___ Measure nose and compare to
measurement made at start of year.

SATdownallday ___ Have a V. Nice weekend if poss.

FUNday (we hope) ___

DIARY

MONTH: YEAR 199_

Moanday ___   Only ONE more page to go...

Chewsday ___   Ask yourself: Has it been
FUN?

Wensdy — ◯ ← Fill in sad or happy face.

Thirsty ___

Frydy ___

SATdownallday ___ Have another V. Nice weekend
if poss.

FUNday (we hope) ___ **CHEERIO** Have a V. Nice
year next year!

Lists of favourite, nice, helpful

NAME: Louise Pride

ADDDRESS: 19, Ploughmans Walk
Stoke Heathe
Bromsgrove.

Tel: (01527) 830684

NAME: Hannah Bamby

ADDDRESS: Bartford cottage
Hambury

Tel: (01524) 821642

NAME: Kirsty Bridgewater

ADDDRESS: 11, Cherry Orch. Drive
Bromsgrove

Tel: (01527) 574202

NAME: Sophie Barford

ADDDRESS:

Dodford

Tel: (01527)

NAME: Amanda Silver

ADDDRESS:

Tel:

NAME: Anna-Louise Cooke

ADDDRESS:

Tel:

Kind people. Etck.

NAME: Lindsay Pearman

ADDDRESS:

Tel:
_____

NAME:

ADDDRESS:

Tel:
_____

NAME:

ADDDRESS:

Tel:
_____

NAME:

ADDDRESS:

Tel:
_____

NAME:

ADDDRESS:

Tel:
_____

NAME:

ADDDRESS:

Tel:
_____

Nosey Parkers keep OUT!

NAME:
ADDDRESS:

Tel:
NAME:
ADDDRESS:

Tel:
NAME:
ADDDRESS:

Tel:
NAME:
ADDDRESS:

Tel:
NAME:
ADDDRESS:

Tel:
NAME:
ADDDRESS:

Tel:

TEENAGE WORRIER'S FRIENDS' FRENDZ

NAME:

ADDDRESS:

Tel:

NAME:

ADDDRESS:

Tel:

NAME:

ADDDRESS:

Tel:

NAME:

ADDDRESS:

Tel:

NAME:

ADDDRESS:

Tel:

NAME:

ADDDRESS:

Tel:

why hasn't she put me down in here?

Cos I would NEVER put Rover down, ever

TEENAGE WORRIER'S FRIEND

NAME:
ADDDRESS:

Tel:
NAME:
ADDDRESS:

Tel:
NAME:
ADDDRESS:

Tel:
NAME:
ADDDRESS:

Tel:
NAME:
ADDDRESS:

Tel:
NAME:
ADDDRESS:

Tel:

Er, I have got Frendz of course
but I seem to have filled MY own
copy of this DIARY with my DOCTOR, Local Health Clinic, Hospital, Emergency Tel nos. Etck Etck.

WORRY WORRY WORRY WORRY

NAME:

ADDDRESS:

Tel:

NAME:

ADDDRESS:

Tel:

NAME:

ADDDRESS:

Tel:

NAME:

ADDDRESS:

Tel:

NAME:

ADDDRESS:

Tel:

NAME:

ADDDRESS:

Tel:

AGITPROP ← A phrase my father uses, meaning 'AGITation & PROPaganda'

TOP BRASS

V. Powerful People to complain to (about rich getting richer, poor getting poorer, Nasty World Etck.)

The Queen
Buckingham Palace
London SW1
0171 930 4832

NB. As a result of my last book "I WAS A TEENAGE WORRIER" the Queen now pays taxes. So you CAN change World.

Prime Minister
10 Downing Street
London SW1
0171 270 3000 ←

(John Major at time of writing but who knows what will happen Etck)
this isn't the no. for Downing Street, but it's the PM's office no. at the House of Commons

Your MP ← Write to this person (ie Member for Sutton West) about Local probs. ie. Litter, not eNuf Trees Too many exams Etck.
House of Commons
London SW1
0171 219 3000

Your Unelected Representative
House of Lords
London SW1
0171 219 3000

Minister of Education *(Boo hoo or boo hiss)*
Department of Education and Science
Sanctuary Building ← will be needing sanctuary v. soon from hordes of teachers, Pupils, Parents Etck.
Great Smith Street
London SW1P 3BT
0171 925 5000

Health Sec *Virginia Bottomley at time of writing,*
Department of Health and Social Security *but just as they*
Richmond House *learn about the job,*
79 Whitehall *Ministers are moved on.*
London SW1 *COMPLAIN about NO free*
0171 210 3000 *eye tests for pensioners,*
decline of NHS
Etck Etck.

Department of Trade and Industry
Ashdown House
Victoria Street ↑
London SW1 *Wot INDUSTRY?*
0171 215 5000

Department of the Environment ← *Moan to this lot*
2 Marshan Street *about PRIVATISED trains,*
London SW1P 3EB *horrible cars, no parks,*
0171 276 0900 *dog poo, lack of Fun*
for Yoof Etck. Etck.

President of USA *(currently Bill Clinton)*
The White House
Washington DC ← *More Levis,*
USA *less GUNS.*
001 202 456 1414

Russian President *(Boris Yeltsin right now)*
Red Square *Wot is*
Moscow *happening?*
Russia *Arg.*
00 7095 925 9051

POLITICAL PARTIES

Communist Party of Great Britain ← *yes! It still exists*
3 Ardleigh Road
London N1
0171 275 8162

TEENAGE WORRIER'S FRIEND

Conservative Central Office
32 Smith Square
London SW1 3HH
0171 222 9000

I hear there are still some of these, too.

(Young Conservatives at this address and no. too)

The Green Party
10 Station Parade
Balham High Road
London SW12 9AZ
0181 673 0045

Labour Party Head Office
150 Walworth Road
London SE17 1JL
0171 710 1234

"What do we want?" "SOMETHING" "When do we want it?" "NOW!"

Labour Students   *(but includes all young people. Phew.*
Same address   *Wot a relief, you don't have to take out*
0171 234 3364   *a student loan to join)*

Liberal Democrats H/Q
4 Cowley Street
London SW1P 3NB
0171 222 7999

BRING BACK THE CAT

Social Democratic Party (SDP)
28 Buckingham Gate
London SW1E 6LD
0171 630 1908

Young Social and Liberal Democrats of England
4 Cowley Street
London SW1P 3NB
0171 233 0675

POLITICAL/PRESSURE GROUPS

300 Group
3rd Floor
19 Borough High Street
London SE1 9SE
0171 357 6660

*Campaign to bring more women
into Parl. and encourage women
in general. Go to schools. V. keen
to catch them young.*

You can write to Political Prisoners all over the World through them.

Amnesty International
99 Roseberry Avenue
London EC1R 4RE
0171 814 6200

*(Has youth section at same address –
has special publication for youth
NEW RELEASE twice yearly –
aimed at teenagers)*

Anti-Apartheid Movement
13 Mandela Street
London NW1
0171 387 7966

GUILT about not doing enough for WORLD Etck Etck

Article 19
90 Borough High Street
London SE1 8QH
0171 403 4822

*– human rights organisation for
freedom of expression*

CND *(Campaign for Nuclear Disarmament)*
162 Holloway Road
London N7 8DQ
0171 700 2393
(Youth CND in same office)

Electoral Reform Society
6 Chancel Street
London SE1 0UU
0171 928 1622

*– proportional representation
and associated democratic aims*

TEENAGE WORRIER'S FRIEND

European Movement
158 Buckingham Palace road
London SW1
0171 824 8388

*Maastricht,
know what
I mean?*

AIDS

Positive Youth
c/o Body Positive
51b Philbeach Gdns
London SW5 9EB
0171 373 7547

0171 373 9124

*— has regular meetings for
young people*

*— information and advice for
people under 25*

— helpline

Positively Women
5 Sebastian Street
London EC1
0171 490 5515
0171 490 5501

*N.B. Oily spermkides
(or even hand cream!)
can dissolve condoms.
Always use a water-
based one. (if you are
DOING IT, Moan whinge)*

The Terrence Higgins Trust
52-54 Grays Inn Rd
London WC1
0171 831 0330
0171 242 1010 – helpline

*— mainly aimed at
homosexuals with HIV and
AIDS (but will help anybody)*

ALCOHOL

Alateen
61 Great Dover Street
London SE1 4YF
0171 403 0888

*Part of Al-Anon – for relatives
of alcholics (and is at the same
address). It is Al-Anon's section
for young people (12-20). There
are organisations all around the country)*

Alcoholics Anonymous *(if you have a problem)*
PO Box 1
Stonebow House
York
01904 644026

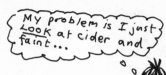

My problem is I just LOOK at cider and faint...

"ALTERNATIVE HEALTH"

Institute for Complementary Medicine
Unit 4
Tavern Quay
Plough Way
London SE16
0171 237 5165

Er, this doesn't mean you get docs who say "Goodness, You're a clever, pleasant person". It means a different, EXTRA, approach to Health.

Society of Homoeopaths
2 Artisan Road
Northampton NN1 4HU
01604 21400

ANIMALS/BIRDS/REPTILES

Cat's Protection League
17 King's Road
Horsham
W. Sussex RH13 5PN
01403 261947

No org. for Dinosaurs yet. But Dr. Spielberg is working on it

International League for the Protection of Horses (H/Q)
Anne Colvin House
Snetterton
Norfolk
01953 498682

TEENAGE WORRIER'S FRIEND

League Against Cruel Sports Ltd
83 Union Street
London SE1
0171 407 0979
0171 403 6155

← "The unspeakable in Pursuit of the Uneatable" as ye great Oscar Wilde noted.

National Canine Defence League
1 Pratt Mews
London NW1 0AD
0171 388 0137

← Don't tell my cat Rover that I put this one in.

Royal Society for the Protection of Birds
The Lodge
Sandy
Beds SG19 2DL
01767 680551

Runs a young ornithologists club

↖ Er, or this one

Royal Society for the Prevention of Cruelty to Animals
(RSPCA)
Causeway
Horsham
W Sussex RH12 1HG
01403 264181

Animal Action Club for under 17s, magazine Animal World, *folder, badge Etck*

World Society for the Protection of Animals
2 Langley Lane
London SW8
0171 793 0540

 # ARTS Etck

Arts Council
14 Gt Peter Street
London SW1P 3NQ
0171 333 0100

Youth funding for youth initiative. Not V. helpful when I rang, but can give info on what orgs they fund for youth

V. USEFUL ADDRESSES

British Film Institute
21 Stephen Street
London W1P 1PL
0171 255 1444

Can put you in touch with
courses in your area

N.B. Campaign for FILM JOBZ.

otherwise V. talented young directors, like Moi, will be PENNILESS.

NAYT (National Association of Youth Theatres)
Unit 1304
The Custard Factory
Gibb Street
Digbeth
Birmingham B9 4AA
0121 608 2111

N.B. All these are NATIONAL orgs but shld be able to put you in touch with Local groups Etck.

National Trust for Places of
Historic Interest and Beauty
36 Queen Anne's Gate
London SW1H 9AS
0171 222 9251

Lots of activities, Young NT,
newsletter, competitions Etck

National Youth Jazz Association
11 Victor Road
Harrow
0181 863 2717

For 11- to 25-year-olds.
Anyone can turn up and play
in orchestra – no audition
required. Can give addresses
round country for jazz

National Youth Orchestra of Great Britain
Causeway House
Lodge Causeway
Fishponds
Bristol
0117 965 0036

Really for super-gifted Grade 8
distinction people under 18.
But they can give info to
everybody about orchestral
things all over country

TEENAGE WORRIER'S FRIEND

National Youth Theatre of Great Britain
443 Holloway Road
London N7 6LW
0171 281 8246

14-21. Daniel Day-Lewis, Timothy Dalton, Ben Kingsley, Simon Ward, Alfred Molina. and Kate Adie went here. Auditions held all round country for holiday productions. Token fee for auditions/interview. Apparently character more important than ability. (They can help with grants for those who can't afford it.) Hoping to set up workshops round country for budding actors

N.B. If you've heard of any of these people, then this could be the place for you.
(I have, of course, ahem, and am a V. Great Supporter of theatre, and Culcher with a capital 'C' Etck instead of V. BORING TV).

Royal Photographic Society
The Octagon
Milsom Street
Bath BA1 1DN
01225 462841

Special discounts for young people. They can put you in contact with regional organisers for workshops, courses Etck

Young Musicians Symphony Ochestra
4-11 Gunnersbury Ave
London W5 3NJ
0181 993 3135

Youth and Music
28 Charing Cross Road
London WC2H 0DB
0171 379 6722

For membership fee of £14 (London) or £7 (elsewhere) you get stage pass which gives you discount tickets to 14 to 30-year-olds for various theatres, concerts Etck

Youth Arts Directory
c/o National Youth Agency
17-23 Albion Street
Leicester LE1 6ED
01533 471200

*Directory lists youth
arts groups around country.
NB The National Youth
Agency can't help you, you
need the directory*

Youth Clubs UK
11 St Bride Street
London EC4
0171 353 2366

*Umbrella org – can give info
on your local youth club.
For 8 to 24-year-olds*

BROADCASTING SERVICES

BBC
Broadcasting House
Portland Place
London W1A 1AA
0171 580 4468

BBC World Service
PO Box 76
Bush House
Strand WC2B
0171 257 2775

BBC TV
Television Centre
Wood Lane
London W12 7RJ
0181 743 8000

*BBC have studios all around, but if you ring this no. you will be put
through to whichever programme you want – eventually*

TEENAGE WORRIER'S FRIEND

Channel 4
60 Charlotte Street
London W1P 2AX
0171 631 4444

ITN (Independent Television News)
200 Gray's Inn Road
London WC1X 8XZ
0171 833 3000

(Channel 4 news at same address)

Loads of separate Franchise companies for radio and TV, but on of the above should put you in touch

❗ CHARACTER-BULDING ORGS

Adventure Service Challenge
87 The Grove
Isleworth
Middx TW7 4JD
0181 560 0079

For 8-15 age-group. Encourages young people to see life as an adventure. Runs activity scheme. Prepares for Duke of Edinburgh awards

Air Training Corps
Headquarters Air Cadets
RAF Newton
Nottingham NG1 8HR
01949 20771

Fosters spirit of adventure, leadership skills, good citizenship blah blah blah. Open to young women, men 13-22. lots of activities eg annual holiday camps

V. USEFUL ADDRESSES

Cirdan Trust
Fullbridge Wharf
Maldon
Essex CM9 7LE
01621 851433

Provides training and instruction on sailing large vessels. 10 to early 20s. Anyone from youth org in widest context (eg school) eligible

Duke of Edinburgh Award Scheme
Gulliver House
Madeira Walk
Windsor
Berks, SQ4 1EU
01753 810753

14-25s eligible. Bronze, silver and gold awards for doing lots of character-building things like going for long walks, taking up new hobbies, visiting old people

Fairbridge
5 Westminster Bridge Road
London SE1 7XW
0171 928 1704

Helps young people aged 14 plus esp. from inner city areas

Outward Bound Trust
Chestnut Field
Regent Place
Rugby
Warks CV21 2PJ
01788 560423

Minimum age: 14

Sea Cadet Corps
202 Lambeth Road
London SE1 7JF
0171 928 8978

Ages 12-18

ArGH! WiSH I'd LEARNT how to do this

TEENAGE WORRIER'S FRIEND

Sea Ranger Association
HQTS Lord Amory
Dollar Bay
301 Marsh Wall
London E14 9TF
0171 987 1757

To promote instruction and training to girls of all races and creeds

CLEVER TEENAGE WORRIERS

Able Publications
Caxton Villa
Park Lane
Knebworth
Herts SG3 6EX
01438 812320

Publishes things for clever people

Gifted Children's Information Centre
Hampton Grange
21 Hampton Lane
Solihull B91 2QJ
0121 705 4547

Offers free telephone counselling for children

MENSA
Bond House
St John's Square
Wolverhampton
01902 772771

If you are V. BRAINY, or just like IQ Tests (not a v. good indication of Intelligence in my Humble opinion - as I enjoy them myself) Then This is the PAGE for You

↑
My brain

↑
pea

V. USEFUL ADDRESSES

National Association of Gifted Children
Park Campus   *Arranges activities for teenagers*
Boughton Green Road
Northampton NN2 7AL
01604 792300

Potential Trust and Questors   *Provides activities and*
7 Bateman Street   *residential weekends for v.*
Headington   *brainy teenagers*
Oxford OX3 7BG
01865 750360

DIVORCE

Argh! Major WORRY if you are lucky enough to have 2 Married parents!

National Stepfamily Association
72 Willesden Lane   *Offers counselling service*
London NW6 7TA   *for everyone having probs.*
0171 372 0844   *Membership includes newsletter*
0171 372 0846   *for children. Also have a v.*
                        useful leaflet for teenagers

DRUGS

ADFAM National   *For family and friends of*
1st Floor   *drug users*
Chapel House
Hatton Place
London EC1N 8ND
0171 405 3923

Drugline
Drug Advisory Centre
9a Brockley X
London SE4 2AB
0181 692 4975

I am so worried I might be offered ILLEGAL substances that I am the only HYPOCHONDRIAC in history to turn down hot lemon from a stranger.

TEENAGE WORRIER'S FRIEND

Re-solve – solvent *(inhalable things)* abuse
30a High Street
Stone
Staffordshire ST15 8AW
01785 817885

Although it's for everybody,
substance abuse is mainly a
young people problem

Release
(Criminal Legal & Drugs Service)
388 Old Street
London EC1V 9LT
0171 729 9904
0171 603 8654 – *24 hour helpline*

SCODA
(Standing Conference
on Drug Abuse)
1-4 Hatton Place,
London EC1 8ND
0171 430 2341

Phone operator and ask for Free
Phone Drug Problems. This will give
the no. of a 24-hour recorded delivery
message which will give you a local
no. you can ring for advice. During
working hours, SKODA can give
you no. themselves

More Drug Stuff

ENVIRONMENTAL

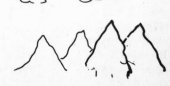

Friends of the Earth
26 Underwood Street
London N1 7JT
0171 490 1555

Earth Action
56 Alma Street
Luton LU1 2PH
01582 482297

Greenpeace UK
Canonbury Villas
London N1 2PN
0171 354 5100

TOO EXHAUSTED to walk?

GENERAL PROBLEMS, BULLYING ETCK

Anti-Bullying Campaign
Room 37
10 Borough High Street
London SE1
071 378 1446/7/8/9

← We could certainly do with some help from this LOT at Sluggs Comprehensive.

British Youth Council
57 Chalton Street
London NW1
0171 387 7559

Represents youth interests.
Loads of socs. attached to it.
Meets gov. ministers to talk
about youth issues

Childline
2nd Floor
Royal Mail Building
Studd Street
London N1 0QW
0800 1111 – *freephone*

← If you or a friend have been SEXUALLY ABUSED these people should be v. helpful and sympathetic

Youth Access
Magazine Business Centre
11 Newark Street
Leicester LE1 5SS
0116 255 8763

Deals with any problem.
Puts young people in touch
with an org (or person)
local to them which can help

TEENAGE WORRIER'S FRIEND

LAW

The Children's Legal Centre
20 Compton Terrace
London N1 2UN
0171 359 6251

Also know about Fast-disappearing ↓ Legal Aid.

National Assocation of Citizens Advice Bureaux
136-144 City Road
London EC1V
0171 251 2000

(They will give you the address/no. of your local CAB, or look in phone bk.) All volunteers are trained. Know all about debt, law, benefits, housing Etck – and know about specific youth things too

National Council of Civil Liberties (NCCL)
21 Tabard Street
London SE1 4LA
0171 403 3888

 ## LESBIAN AND GAY

As far as I know, I am not a Lesbian but it seems to be V. common so don't be shy.

Lesbian and Gay Switchboard
BM Switchboard
London N1 9PT
0171 837 7324

V. hard to get through on this no. according to my friend Hazel **But KEEP trying !!**

North London Lesbian and Gay Project
0171 607 8346

They're only called this because they're financed by Islington – really a national young person's organisation (under 25s). Arrange pen pals etck. They don't give out address because it's been abused in the past.

Lesbian and Gay local lines in phone books are a good bet.

MANNERS

They are V. Polite on the phone ←

Polite Society
6 Norman Avenue
Henley-on-Thames
Oxfordshire BG9 1SG
01491 572794

To preserve and maintain good manners as the foundation for British Society

← *couldn't resist this as my baby brother BENJY could do with their help. (NOT moi, of COURSE).*

NATIONAL NEWSPAPERS

Morning

These are the 'opinion Formers' so they say. So they are worth LOBBYING etck.

Daily Express
Ludgate House
245 Blackfriars Road
London SE1 9UF
0171 928 8000

Daily Mail
Northcliffe House
2 Derry Street
London W8 5HY
0171 938 6000

Daily Mirror
1 Canada Square
London E14 5AD
0171 510 3000

↑ This is not a Newspaper

TEENAGE WORRIER'S FRIEND

Daily Telegraph
South Quay Plaza
181 Marsh Wall
London E14 5DT
0171 538 5000

Financial Times
Number One
Southwark Bridge
London SE1 1XX
0171 873 3000

The Guardian
119 Farringdon Road
London EC1R 3ER
0171 278 2332

The Independent
40 City Road
london EC1Y 2DB
0171 253 1222

Morning Star
1-3 Ardleigh Road
London N1 4HS
0171 254 0033

The Sun
1 Virginia Street
London E1 9XP
0171 782 4000

The Times
1 Virginia Street
London E1 9XN
0171 782 5000

You could always try to persuade the adults in your life not to read these V. Trashy comics (although the big papers are less Trashy than the little ones). There are SOME (i mention no names) who make The Beano seem like Shakespeare.

Today
1 Virginia Street
London E1 9BD
0171 782 4600

Sunday

Independent on Sunday
40 City Road
London EC1Y 2DB
0171 253 1222

The Mail on Sunday
Northcliffe House
2 Derry Street
London W8 5EE
0171 938 6000

News of the World
Admiral's House
1 Virginia Street
London E19 6XJ
0171 782 4000

Observer
119 Farringdon Road
London EC1R 3ER
0171 278 2332

Sunday Express
Ludgate House
245 Blackfriars Road
London SE1 9UF
0171 928 8000

You will notice also that almost all the 'Newspapers' in Britain support the Conservative party. In the mid-term of a Government they will attack it, sometimes quite hard. But just B4 an Election they will see this nobble, er, I mean noble, Party's excellent attributes and rush, courageously, to its side.

TEENAGE WORRIER'S FRIEND

Sunday Mirror
1 Canada Square
London E14 5AD
0171 510 3000

The People
1 Canada Square
London E14 5AD
0171 510 3000

Sunday Telegraph
South Quay Plaza
181 Marsh Wall
London E14 5DT
0171 538 5000

Sunday Times
1 Virginia Street
London E1 9XW
0171 782 5000

Sunday Sport
39-46 East Road
London N1 6AH
0171 251 2544

Still, Journalists have a V. Nice life with big LUNCHES Etck so they can Laugh at the rest of us and do not care if we Fume, Etck.

Maybe I'll be a Hack myself if film directing falls through. Fearless Investigative stuff of course, ahem.

PREGNANCY/CONTRACEPTION

British Pregnancy Advisory Service
7 Belgrave Road
London SW1
0171 222 0985

Check out your spermicide! (see AIDS) ooo whoops?

Brook Advisory Centres   *Young men are welcome too*
National Office
153a East Street
London SE17 2SD
0171 708 1234 *(general enquiries)*
0171 708 1390 *(press and publications)*
0171 617 8000 *(recorded information helpline giving immediate info
on contraception, abortion, pregnancy testing, STDs Etck.)*

Family Planning Assocation
27 Mortimer Street
London W1N 7RJ
0171 636 7866

RELIGION

Campaign for Nun-Employment

Archbishop of Canterbury
Lambeth Palace
London SE1 7JU
0171 928 8282

Cardinal Hume
Archbishop's House
Ambrosden House
London SW1P
0171 834 1717

TEENAGE WORRIER'S FRIEND

Clergy House
42 Francis Street
London SW1P 1QW
0171 834 7452

Administrative centre of Catholic Church

Islamic Cultural Centre
Regents Park
146 Park Road
London NW8
0171 724 3363

They don't have a head in this country. This centre can put you in touch with youth orgs. on the UK

The Pope
The Vatican
00 396 6982

Q: What fun does the Pope have?
A: Nun

Dr Jonathan Sacks
Office of the Chief Rabbi
Alder House
Tavistock Square
London WC1H
0171 387 1066

This office can put you in touch with youth orgs.

The Salvation Army
101 Queen Victoria Street
London EC4P
0171 236 5222

Of course there are loads of other Religious groups. I am going to be a Bhuddist myself. I think...

Youth Section
The Salvation Army
William Booth Memorial
   Training College
Denmark Hill
London SE5 8BQ
0171 738 5533

Offers help and support with all sorts of things

USEFUL ORGANISATIONS WHICH HAVE RELIGIOUS CONNOTATIONS BUT WHICH AREN'T REALLY CONNECTED TO CHURCH ANY MORE:

Children's Society Headquarters
  (used to be Church of England
  Children's Society)
Edward Rudolf House   *Runs projects up and down*
Margery Street   *country. Counselling, youth*
London WC1X 0JL   *clubs, legal advice, coping*
0171 837 4299   *with parental divorce etck*

Guides Association   *Can put you in touch*
17-19 Buckingham Palace Road *with local orgs*
London SW1W 0PT
0171 834 6242

Scout Association   *Ditto* or
Baden-Powell House   Dib -dib.
Queen's Gate   or Ging gang
London SW7 5JB   gooly ....
0171 584 7030

YWCA Headquarters   *For 13-up. Youth and community*
Clarendon House   *centres, sport adventure weekends.*
52 Cornmarket Street   *V. helpful to young mothers of*
Oxford OX1 3EJ   *school age and ethnic minorities.*
01865 726110   *Christian element is there – but*
                          only if you want it

RUNAWAYS

The Piccadilly Advice Centre
100 Shaftesbury Avenue
London W1
0171 434 3773

*This is a safe house for
runaways – passes on
messages without saying
where runaways are*

SPORTS

ARCHERY
Grand National Archery Society
Tel: 01203 696631

ATHLETICS
Athletics Assocation of England
Tel: 0121 440 5000

BADMINTON
Badminton Assocation of England
Tel: 01908 568822

BASEBALL
British Baseball Assocation of England
Tel: 01482 643551

BASKETBALL
English Basketball Federation Ltd.
Tel: 0113 261166

BILLIARDS AND SNOOKER
World Professional Billiard and Snooker Assoc
0117 974 4491

oh Dear, rather a lot of SPORT. Next time I'll do Etching, Pottery, Papier Maché, Etck Etck. But see ARTS

CAMPING AND CARAVANNING
Camping and Caravanning Club
Tel: 01203 694995

CANOEING
British Canoe Union
Tel: 0115 982110

CAVING
National Caving Association
Tel: 01639 849519

CRICKET
National Cricket Association
Tel: 0171 289 6098

CRICKET (WOMEN)
Women's Cricket Association
Tel: 0121 440 0520

CROQUET
The Croquet Association
Tel: 0171 736 3148

CYCLING
British Cycle Federation
Tel: 01536 412211

British Cycle Speedway Council
Tel: 01508 63880

Cyclist's Touring Club
Tel: 01483 417217

some people's idea of FUN...

O.K. I'm not V. Sporty since not being encouraged in FOOTBALL at which I was once a budding GENIUS

TEENAGE WORRIER'S FRIEND

British Mountain Bike Federation
01536 412211

DISABLED (Sports for)
British Sports Association for the Disabled
0171 490 4919

FENCING
Amateur Fencing Association
Tel: 0181 742 3032

FOOTBALL
Football Association
Tel: 0171 262 4542

FOOTBALL (WOMEN'S)
Women's Football Association
Tel: 01707 651840

GOLF
English Golf Union
Tel: 0113 255 3042

GOLF (WOMEN)
English Ladies' Golf Association
Tel: 0121 456 2088

GYMNASTICS
British Amateur Gymnastics Association
Tel: 01952 820330

CAMPAIGN FOR GIRLS' SOCCER AT SCHOOL!

NOT ABOUT FELINE FOOTBALL

HANDBALL
British Handball Association
Tel: 01706 229354

HOCKEY
The Hockey Association
Tel: 01908 241100

All England Women's Hockey Association
Tel: 01743 233572

England Mixed Hockey Association
0171 377 9750

ICE HOCKEY
British Ice Hockey Association
Tel: 01202 303946

JOGGING
National Jogging Association
Tel: 01623 793496

JUDO
British Judo Association
Tel: 0116 2559669

KEEP FIT
Keep Fit Association
0171 233 8898

TEENAGE WORRIER'S FRIEND

LACROSSE (WO<del>MEN'S</del>)

All England Women's Lacrosse Association
Tel: 0121 773 4422

Lacrosse
(yeeech)
arg

LAWN TENNIS
Lawn Tennis Association
Tel: 0171 381 7000

MARTIAL ARTS
British Aikido Board
Tel: 01753 819086

English Karate Governing Board
Tel: 01225 834008

British Kendo Association
Tel: 01543 466334

If you play
this, please
write and tell
me what it is.

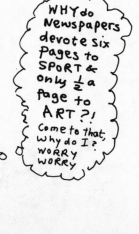

WHY do Newspapers devote six pages to SPORT & only ½ a page to ART ?! Come to that, why do I? WORRY WORRY

MODERN PENTATHLON
Modern Pentathlon Association of Great Britain
Tel: 01747 855833

MOUNTAINEERING
British Mountaineering Council
Tel: 0161 273 5835

MOVEMENT AND DANCE
British Council of Ballroom Dancing
Tel: 0171 609 1386

English Amateur Dancers Association
Tel: 0171 636 0851

NETBALL
All England Netball Association
Tel: 01462 442344

ORIENTEERING
British Orienteering Federation
Tel: 01629 734042

PETANQUE
British Petanque Association
Tel: 01203 421408

POOL
English Pool association
Tel: 01922 35587

TEENAGE WORRIER'S FRIEND

RACKETBALL
British racketball Association
Tel: 01322 272200

RAMBLING
The Ramblers Association
Tel: 0171 582 6878

RIDING
British Horse Society
Tel: 01203 696697

ROLLER HOCKEY
National Roller Hockey Association of England
Tel; 01622 743155

ROLLER SKATING
British Federation of Roller Skating
Tel: 01952 825253

ROUNDERS
National Rounders Association
Tel: 01602 785514

ROWING
Amateur Rowing Association
Tel: 0181 748 3632

RUGBY LEAGUE
British Amateur Rugby League Association
Tel: 01484 544131

Oh well. SOME OF you are V. sporty ...aren't you??

Here's one I like! Wish I could afford it moan whinge

SAILING
Royal Yachting Association
Tel: 01703 629962

British Federation of Sand and Land Yacht Clubs
Tel: 01509 842292

SKATING
National Ice Skating Association of Great Britain
Tel: 0171 253 3824

SKIING
English Ski Council
Tel: 0121 501 2314

SOFTBALL
British Softball Federation
Tel: 01737 765 303 (home)
01737 765457 (work)

SQUASH (MEN & WOMEN)
Squash Rackets Association
Tel: 0181 746 1616

SUB AQUA
The British Sub Aqua Club
Tel: 0151 357 1951

SURFING
British Surfing Association
Tel: 01736 60250

TEENAGE WORRIER'S FRIEND

SWIMMING
Amateur Swimming Association
Tel: 01509 230431

TABLE TENNIS
English Table Tennis Association
Tel: 01424 722525

TCHOUK BALL
British Tchouk Ball Association
Tel: 01242 231154

TOBOGGANING
The GB Luge Association
Tel: 01432 353920 (work)

TRAMPOLINING
British Trampoline Federation
Tel: 0181 863 7278

VOLLEYBALL
English Volleyball Association
Tel: 0115 9816324

WATER SKIING
British Water Ski Federation
Tel: 0171 833 2855

WEIGHT LIFTING
British amateur Weight Lifting
Tel: 01865 778319

Actually, I feel so fit after reading all these that I do not feel the NEED to, er, engage in any of these V. useful and um, fittening activities

YOGA
British Wheel of Yoga
Tel: 0181 598 4360 (work)

TRAVEL

Student Travel Centre
18 Rupert Street
London W1V
0171 434 1306

Reduced prices for young people

Youth Hostels Association
(England and Wales)
14 Southampton Way
London WC2 7HY
0171 836 1036 (Membership)

*Members have to be 14
to go hostelling.*

8 St Stephens Hill
St Albans
Herts AL1 2DY
01727 855215 (head office)

YHA Scotland
7 Glebe crescent
Stirling SK8 2JA
01786 451181

TEENAGE WORRIER'S FRIEND
VEGETARIAN

Beauty Without Cruelty   *Cruelty-free list, product guide*
57 King Henry's Walk   *Etck*
London N1
0171 254 2929

British Union for the Abolition of Vivisection
16a Crane Grove   *Free packs for over-11s*
London N7
0171 700 4888

Vegan Society
7 Battle Road
St Leonards-on-Sea
East Sussex TN37 7AA
01424 427393

Vegetarian Society UK Ltd,   *Recipes, resource packs,*
Parkdale   *quarterly mag for young*
Dunham Road   *people* Green Scene
Altringham
Cheshire WA14 4QG
0161 928 0793

Yes! chips are Vegetables!

But do APPLES cry when you PICK them? WORRY WORRY WORRY

sometimes, I feel so alone...

TEENAGE THINK TANK

WORRIERS OF THE WORLD UNITE!

This is a plea from the Letty Chubb Campaign for JOB SWAPS.

We would like to ask all EMPLOYED adults to give one day's work (for one half-a-day's pay) to UNEMPLOYED Youth, each week.

TEENAGE WORRIERS

are V.V.V.V. Worried about the future for British Youth and would like to point out that we need MONEY (er, and TRAINING and EXPERIENCE, Etck) in order to KEEP US OFF THE STREETS (er, and give us selfesteem and enable us to help the future of this once great Nation).

We would also like to campaign for a **TEENAGE THINK TANK** to help save the Planet. Etck. Please bring this up with

PTO

your Local Constituency Party.
And the Prime Minister.

Names	Addresses

To Letty Chubb
c/o Piccadilly Press
5 Castle Rd
LONDON NW1 8PR

Dear Letty

Please could you
write a book about....

Here's what I thought about
your diary...

Here's what I thought about
I WAS A TEENAGE WORRIER.

Can you campaign for ....

Love from

The End

—

cat s a REZ
Okay